SEASONS AT LAKESIDE DAIRY

Lakeside Dairy branding iron (AB), Myles L. Collins, photographer.

ATLANTIC
MIGRATIONS
— AND THE —
AFRICAN
DIASPORA

JESSICA B. HARRIS, SERIES EDITOR

SEASONS AT
LAKESIDE
DAIRY

Family Stories from a Black-Owned Dairy,
Louisiana to California and Beyond

Lizzetta LeFalle-Collins

University Press of Mississippi / Jackson

The University Press of Mississippi is the scholarly publishing agency of the Mississippi Institutions of Higher Learning: Alcorn State University, Delta State University, Jackson State University, Mississippi State University, Mississippi University for Women, Mississippi Valley State University, University of Mississippi, and University of Southern Mississippi.

www.upress.state.ms.us

The University Press of Mississippi is a member of the Association of University Presses.

Photographs are courtesy of the author unless otherwise noted.

Library of Congress Cataloging-in-Publication Data

Names: LeFalle-Collins, Lizzetta, author.
Title: Seasons at Lakeside Dairy : family stories from a Black-owned dairy, Louisiana to California and beyond / Lizzetta LeFalle-Collins.
Other titles: Atlantic migrations and the African diaspora.
Description: Jackson : University Press of Mississippi, 2024. | Series: Atlantic migrations and the African diaspora | Includes bibliographical references.
Identifiers: LCCN 2024010598 (print) | LCCN 2024010599 (ebook) | ISBN 9781496852090 (hardback) | ISBN 9781496852083 (epub) | ISBN 9781496852076 (epub) | ISBN 9781496852069 (pdf) | ISBN 9781496852052 (pdf)
Subjects: LCSH: Bates family. | Bates, Angus. | Lakeside Dairy. | African American families—History. | Dairy farms—Louisiana. | Dairy farming—Louisiana. | Cookbooks—20th century.
Classification: LCC E185.96 L38 2024 (print) | LCC E185.96 (ebook) | DDC 929.20973—dc23/eng/20240422
LC record available at https://lccn.loc.gov/2024010598
LC ebook record available at https://lccn.loc.gov/2024010599

British Library Cataloging-in-Publication Data available

I dedicate this to my mother, Mrs. Eloise Bates LeFalle, and her siblings for their stories, and my husband, Dr. Willie R. Collins, for editing draft after draft of *Seasons at Lakeside Dairy*. Though all are gone, you live in the pages of this book.

CONTENTS

SEASONS AT LAKESIDE DAIRY

INTRODUCTION

OTHER THAN FOOD, HOW DID THESE STORIES FROM LAKESIDE DAIRY translate to my life? Did I even know they would become a part of me? As an adult, I now look back and see that they were a part of me all the time. They taught me to seek and experience more in life and to follow my own path. So, for me, Grandpa was bigger than life, and he was somewhere in my subconscious when it was time for me to speak up and be present.

The book begins in Los Angeles, where most of my family settled after migrating West. It follows my path of discovery from LA to university and finally back to the dairy lands in Shreveport, Louisiana, where my grandparents ran the dairy and raised their children.

Seasons at Lakeside Dairy is a creative mixed-genre memoir that blurs genres as if mixing and smudging lines and tonal areas in a drawing or painting. My mother's family, the Bateses, often recounted their lives on the dairy my grandfather, Angus Bates, opened in Shreveport in 1907. A Black dairy farmer in the post-Reconstruction South was rare, and my mother and her siblings loved to share their memories of this time and place with anyone who showed an interest in listening. I translated oral storytelling, which fluidly changes from generation to generation, into a hybrid, creative work. These written interpretations are from multiple voices about their family, the dairy lands, and migration West. My relatives' memories were shaped by their birth order in the family. With fourteen (two from a previous marriage) children, their years' range includes multiple viewpoints.

Growing up in Los Angeles, these stories gave me a window into my mother's family's aspirational lives and the seasonal crops and family recipes that sustained them. So naturally, I kept the stories in

3

my memory, later relaying them to my children. When I resumed creative writing, I realized that their stories became my stories, and doors opened to geographic and cultural histories of spaces and landscapes untouched by my pen. Their stories caused me to dig deeper into their abilities to sustain lives of relative economic and social privilege compared to the many Black families who were still under the yoke of the sharecropping system. After reading the histories of Black people during the legacy of Reconstruction in the South, the remaining questions of how my grandfather Angus could sustain a thriving dairy business in such a racially oppressive and hostile environment in northwest Louisiana went unanswered. I kept asking, "How did he do it?" I can only suggest partial answers, perhaps because my family did not reveal the lineage of some secrets. Some topics were too taboo. Their memories centered on daily life at the dairy.

When writing a text that requires interviewing family members, the answers are ripe for interpretation. One member might tell a story one way, in a specific or nonspecific context that deviates from another family member's telling of that story. The stories were rarely tragic, even if there were mysteries to unfold. My refashioned accounts allow me to question events and deviations in the art of storytelling. In writing this book, I admit I heard many memoirs during my youth when they were fresher in the storyteller's memory. Unfortunately, I did not begin writing them down until my family members were considerably older and had foggy recollections. Many of the details had disappeared, and I had to work with fragments of stories. In weaving pieces together, I decided to rely on their voices. I took what I could from their accounts, sometimes remnants I carried around like their scraps of recipes, adjusting them to my tastes.

I researched their historical contexts, embellishing them with fictionalized scenes to excite the senses like any good storyteller. Ultimately, I made them my stories using my creative storytelling and writing skills. I used the same approach with their recipes. In doing so, I brought the recipes into my contemporary life, pairing them with ones I found by celebrated chefs and families posted online. Many recipes that claim to be family recipes or Grandma's recipes are iterations of ones from other sources. Most people put their spins on recipes, giving them another life.

In the beginning, I introduce the reader to the family after they settle in the West, mainly Los Angeles, the San Francisco Bay Area, and

Seattle, Washington, but my focus is on the LA area, my birthplace, and where most of them settled. It was very different for them, taking jobs they did not have to do in Louisiana because the dairy had supported their privileged lifestyle and livelihood. Then, the organization of the text follows the seasons at the dairy. I refer to foods throughout and provide tweaked family recipes culled and interpreted from notes and remembrances of tastes described by family members after each chapter. These recipes illustrate how the family ate and incorporated meat from farm animals, dairy products, and plants they grew and foraged on the dairy's working farm.

Historical research was pertinent to illustrate the character of Grandmother and Grandfather and their beliefs in creating a sustainable life for their children in their semirural community. The main narrative explains why my grandparents decided to stay in the racist and unforgiving South rather than migrate to the North, Midwest, or West during the first migration. The answer is that they owned land, a working dairy, and a home. The land and their ownership of it are critical elements in this story. After researching their lives, oral accounts, and ephemera saved from their home, I surmised that their success as landowners was primarily due to their persistence and embrace of the teachings of two Black men: George Washington Carver (who disseminated innovative recommendations for farmers) and Booker T. Washington (who advocated for Black entrepreneurs to remain and rebuild the South to make it their own). These two men profoundly impacted many Black Southerners, especially in the farming and business communities. While my grandparents stayed in the dairy business on their land and did not participate in the first wave of outward migration of Blacks in the 1920s–1930s, as their children grew older, they understood that times were changing in the industry. The family had to consider how the siblings could sustain themselves if the dairy, their only employer, should close. Several children went away to college or into the armed forces after President Roosevelt desegregated them. But when they returned from college or the service to discover few job prospects, most family members, including my mother, moved west, with one moving to Philadelphia.

Family members' voices punctuate the narrative in passages pulled from interviews with them. Poetry sparked by their words, embedded stories inspired by their storytelling, vintage photographs, and objects from the dairy support the accuracy of the historical narrative. Diverse ephemera and materials illuminate this interpretive memoir about the dairy and the siblings' new Los Angeles community, where they shared culture with other Blacks, primarily from Louisiana and Texas, who had migrated west.

The book charts how the restrictive covenants of the South, the lynching that terrorized families, and the disappointment of many young Black men returning from World War II after fighting for their country all contributed to the downfall of Black businesses in the South. However, the book's most poignant elements are the family members' voices, inserted among the pages as witnesses to a history of successful farm practices often missing in the story of the Great Migration. These voices illustrate a family's joys, hardships, and sorrows while building and managing a family dairy in the segregated South. Their stories of persistence, sustainability, self-sufficiency, and joy are relatable to the struggles of life, the challenges of owning a business, especially a Black dairy with limited clients, an inability to apply for and receive government agricultural loans like White farmers, and the oppressive and unequal treatment by dairy inspectors in present-day rural and urban communities. Additionally, the book does not shy away from discussing roadblocks and limited mobility in housing and employment that Blacks encountered in Los Angeles and how, despite these challenges, the West proved to be a better choice than remaining in the South.

When most of the family settled in Los Angeles, they became a part of a large community of Louisiana transplants. While the narrative is about life on the dairy, it highlights race, class, and color issues among Louisianians and the larger community. It encapsulates the reality of double consciousness, to conform to the dominant White society while embracing their Black selves and culture, needed for survival by aspirational families who became entrepreneurs in the segregated South. I considered the broad range of aesthetic positions Blacks advanced in recognizing their "cultural mulatto" status. On the one hand, they were immersed and indebted to "a multiracial mix of cultures," full of tensions and desires that traversed European and American literary, visual arts, and musical forms.

On the other hand, they presented an alternative view of their brand of Americanness. Their heritage included a history of enslavement and miscegenation, resulting in a double consciousness that sometimes came together in form, content, and materiality. Tensions and desires tore families apart as well as brought them together. Therefore, as much as this book is about my grandparents' dairy land in Shreveport, it extends into many areas, including race and identity, and follows the siblings as they deal with these issues in their migration west.

I began writing *Seasons* over ten years ago. It influenced my creative short story writing; some of those stories appear in this book. My book recalls *The Warmth of Other Suns* by Isabel Wilkerson, who also focuses on migration. However, it differs from Wilkerson's text because I bring an immediate voice and a lived perspective to the migration story as a native of Los Angeles, born at the height of the migration. The pull quotes by family members are matter-of-fact accounts from their lives.

Additionally, a teaching stint at Tuskegee University in Alabama (1979–1984) informed my understanding of the context and influence of the work of George Washington Carver and Booker T. Washington's contributions to the stabilization and success of Black farms in the South, including my mother's family dairy. My grandparents created a home life that helped shape their children's lives. The siblings' first-person inserts help elevate the narrative beyond writing about the environment and create emotionally familiar spaces for others with similar migration stories of leaving home to see themselves.

Further, that foundation carried them as they moved out of the South and settled elsewhere. In rewriting their stories, I placed them in the context of 1930s and '40s Shreveport. I fanned out into their community, notating places, residents, and businesspeople, trying to give a sense of the family's social and historically specific relationships with historical figures they admired. In writing about my relatives, I also told my story as I interacted with them from a young age, detailing how they influenced my outlook on life. In retrospect, my stories also illustrate a period in Los Angeles's history that many ignore. It was not all doom and gloom: Happiness, joy, and rich relationships formed in our small village of migrating Louisianians and Texans.

As a native Angelino, many of my references to Black migrant communities are first-hand observations. My sisters and I were among the first generation of children born to families who migrated to Los Angeles during and after World War II. Migrants wondered if their choices to leave had been the right ones. My youth in LA included an introduction to traditional foodways from my aunts and uncles, who had left their

Southern homes and headed west. Embedded in the narrative is family lore about foods we ate and regularly prepared, adhering to the dairy's seasonal life cycle.

Although this is not a cookbook, I am sharing a selection of recipes to add another sensory experience to help readers understand Lakeside Dairy. Even though I asked my family members questions as they cooked, many of the recipes in this book are interpretations; I often had to go back and check portions with them or ask another relative to chime in to complete the dish. Most times, they did not write recipes down. The food tastes on their tongues determined the amounts of the ingredients. I do not claim a specific recipe from an individual source; my family members cooked, shared, and tasted to arrive at their recipes. My mother taught me how to cook healthy meals to sustain my life. My family's tastes influence my tastes, but I also venture to new flavors and recipes, tasting as I go to create my own. I've written brief contextual statements for selected recipes in each chapter. So, in this book, recipes help combine memories from the dairy land and the new spaces on the West Coast where this Southern family planted new roots.

Finally, *Seasons at Lakeside Dairy* is for anyone who has migrated from home to build a more sustainable life for themselves or their family. We often hear the overarching story of why and how Black families migrated from the Southern United States. This book is for readers interested in memoirs, historical storytelling, and migration stories. The embedded stories are compelling, informative, and humorous as they delve into what it meant to be a Black entrepreneurial farming family during late Reconstruction, one that remained in the South and built a business before joining the great exodus of Blacks into the northern, midwestern, and western cities. But the humanizing narrative of *Seasons at Lakeside Dairy* is the inside story of one family building a thriving business to support fourteen children. In sustaining their family, the heads of the household also helped to support their community. Despite this success, a lack of equity and opportunity pushed the next generation to leave their ancestral home.

MY SEASONS IN LA—STOP AND LISTEN, LOOK TO THE SKY, CAN YOU SMELL THE OCEAN?

Although Shreveport was my mother Eloise Bates LeFalle's home, all but three of her thirteen siblings joined other Louisiana Blacks during a significant exodus from the state to California. They found more employment and educational opportunities and a subtropical climate similar to what they had known in Louisiana. Milk products, field crops, gardens, fruit and nut trees, foraged plants from the woodlands at the edge of the property, and fish and fowl in their "sportsman's paradise" were central to their lives on the dairy farm. This emphasis on gathering, preparing, and eating the local, fresh, seasonal foods that dressed their tables at mealtime and sustained their Southern rural way of life at the dairy continued in Los Angeles. They adapted the agricultural skills they gained from farm work for the city. California provided the space and environment for continued subsistence farming and attendant cultural practices that migrating Louisianans and Texans enjoyed in their home states.

While owning livestock within Los Angeles city limits was illegal, some Southern transplants moved away from the central city to areas like Compton's Richland Farms, finding more agreeable spaces for extensive gardens and farm animals. Griffith Compton donated the land to the County of Los Angeles in 1800 for cultural use. It was a perfect place for many Blacks who preferred country life to settle and raise their families. But, like many other places in the sprawling city and county of LA, it was not developed with large groups of Black folks in mind. My mother had no desire to move into more rural parts of LA because of her experience in Louisiana. Although living on the dairy, "We lived in the town," she said, so after her parents maintained a successful dairy for thirty-six years, she and her migrating siblings chose an urban lifestyle over a rural one. They preferred city life.

Consequently, they chose to live and purchase their homes in the central part of the city, designated for Black homeowners. There, most people grew and maintained manicured lawns and ornamental gardens. Some also practiced subsistence gardening in their back and side yards, planting according to their seasonal schedules in climates similar to their Southern homes. The skills and the resources gained from the dairy business helped my family survive in the urban environment of Los Angeles. Even in the face of an increasingly neglected Black community, my extended family and their village of transplants from Louisiana and Texas created an alternative space to grow and move forward.

My mother's memories of home were related to seasonal changes in Los Angeles, no matter how subtle. They became flashpoints that took her and me to my grandparents' Lakeside Dairy. The seasonal greeting cards my family bought for each other and endearingly distributed, especially for the fall and winter holidays, were always about somewhere else, blanketed with snow, not sunshine. Even the cards with summer scenes with sailboats reminded me of another place. When I went to the beach, I saw surfers riding the waves rather than sailboats. Hallmark card views of the four seasons seemed nonexistent or unrealistic for my LA. They weren't views of LA at all; they were some greeting card designer's concepts of summer. "Los Angeles doesn't have any seasons," I'd often hear visitors say. I'd say, "They don't know LA." "Stop and listen," Mom would say, "look to the sky, feel the changes in the weather, how the wind ruffles the fine hairs on your arms. Hear the birds. Can you smell the ocean?" Mom taught us how to watch the sky, feel the changes in the weather, and notice signs of change. We lived west of downtown in the Chesterfield Square neighborhood, miles from the ocean, but we were far enough west to catch its breezes, marine layer, and sea smell, just like the Westside White folks.

The newspapers and other media referred to where I lived as South-Central LA, a code word for the Black community of Los Angeles. But now it's just South LA. Across the country, covenants redlining Black people out of neighborhoods they could afford were the norm. Consequently, the well-heeled Black, disadvantaged poor, and folks straddling the middle class above and below the median economic line lived in the same neighborhoods. In my village in Los Angeles, we experienced all those economic divides.

HOME IN LA

At our home, the giant California sycamore tree in the parking strip in front of our house was filled with bird activity, acknowledging the changing seasons. Our sycamore undoubtedly reminded my mom of the stately willow in the yard of her family home. Once they settled in Los Angeles, her sisters beautified their front and back yards with plants collected and shared among family members and friends. They rarely purchased plants, not even seeds. Instead, some received seeds from a harvest down south sent with a traveler to LA or by mail. Their love for and propagation of gardens was necessary for sustaining the healthy way of life they had come to love and cherish at home in Louisiana. In addition, it connected them with other members of their Shreveport community who had migrated west.

We watched the giant sycamore tree as a signal of the changing seasons. The tiny lime green buds of the tree, destined to burst into leaves larger than my mom's hand, beckoned warm spring days, especially around Easter Sunday. I looked forward to the warm springs with moderate rain and the church teas with little triangular sandwiches and flowers that decorated the serving plates. The fully opened leaves waved on the outstretched branches as hot summer days greeted us with June gloom, what Angelinos call that cool morning foggy marine layer stretching from Venice Beach to Hollywood.

I remember wearing starched dresses in elementary school. My mother, a housewife and seamstress, made our dresses like her mother made all her children's clothes. Mom always sewed straps on both sides of the waistband of our dresses to tie a big bow in the back that held its shape even when we walked or ran to school. We wore our usually white socks, always folded down just once and very neatly, so if someone took a ruler and measured them on all sides, they measured the same. My two sisters, Jacqueline and Deborah, and I had long, unpressed hair (we didn't get our hair pressed until we went to junior high school or on special occasions). Mom divided our hair into three braids, two at the bottom and one to the side of the top of our heads, pinning them with hairpins. She would tie the ends with bright ribbons so if one fell off, it could easily be seen, curled up on the ground. Then, each weekend, she'd iron them with the other clothes and string the ribbons at the end of her ironing board. We each would retrieve a handful to dress our hair for the coming week. Even now, when I braid and pen my hair with hairpins after a good washing and conditioning, I am momentarily taken back to 1505 West 58th Street, in the backyard, under the apricot tree. This tree provided shade as Mom pulled and tugged, taming our wooly hair.

After braiding our hair, we played one of our favorite games outside while our hair dried. It was one we made up, playing catch by tossing green apricots at each other. When we tired of playing that, we just competed at juggling the apricots. Then Mom sent us up into the tree to pick the ripe ones. We dreaded climbing limb to limb into the leafy tree. We loved eating apricots, but so did bugs. They were okay, but spiders crawled along the branches and made webs between their leaves. Fear of one dropping on me was a constant concern, especially in my newly washed hair. As one of my sisters ascended the tree, the other two stood below to catch the round, light orange fruit. I liked to pick the ones with rosy cheeks. Some even had reddish freckles, which usually meant they were delightfully sweet. We had so much fruit with two apricot trees, even for our family. But my mom was not leaving them to rot on the branches. No, her parents taught her not to waste anything, even free apricots from our trees. We shared them with neighbors because ours were the only apricot trees on the block. But we had plenty left, and we could not eat them fast enough; less, we made multiple trips to the bathroom. So, what do you do with all those apricots? We gave bags to Aunt Lizzetta to make delicious apricot jam. Mom made stewed apricots. She also made apricot pies and shared them with our church in the hospitality room after Sunday service. People loved them, and ladies came up to her, asking not only for her recipe but for apricots. She obliged them, but we still had so many apricots. Mom decided to freeze them.

Our refrigerator freezer was small, but Aunt Lizzetta had a chest freezer, a throwback necessity from life in the South. With so many mouths to feed, my grandparents also had one. People kept them because there was always an overflow of fresh vegetables and fruits free from farmers. Before that, they had an ice box. They gave produce to neighbors rather than turning it into the ground. In the fields and orchards at Lakeside Dairy, the family gathered every bit of salvageable produce and used it in recipes or created new dishes. While I am not a farmer, that trait of food thriftiness runs deep.

Daddy walked us to school. Western Avenue Elementary School had diverse cultures, including Japanese, White, Jewish, Romani, and Black children. There were very few Filipino and Mexican children. Almost all our teachers were White, except for Mrs. Rhone, who was Black and went to our church. My sisters and I befriended several Japanese children. They all took ballet lessons, but when I asked my mom if I could take classes, she said we could not afford them. I was disappointed, but

Mom enrolled all of us in piano lessons on the piano that my Aunt Lizzetta had shipped from their home in Shreveport after Grandma passed. Aunt Lizzetta had no children and was like a second mother to us. Mom probably thought that piano lessons made up for ballet. They did, and what joy we experienced when our piano teacher took us to hear Marion Anderson sing at the Los Angeles Music Center in 1965.

At school, we had special days. The one I remember was a visit from Daisy, the cow. We lived not far from an industrial zone with two dairies, which was part of their education program to get families to drink more milk. Daisy (a real cow) visited our school to help teach us the production of milk. Of course, this was nothing new for my sisters and me because our grandfather had the only Black dairy in Shreveport. So, we already knew about milking cows and making cream, butter, and yogurt. Mother raised us on plain yogurt. The only other flavor available was orange. But we often sweetened plain yogurt with sugar or fruit from our apricot trees. It was a staple in our home because of Mom's experience on her family's dairy farm.

Other special days at school were international days when we dressed in costumes from various countries and did folk dances from those countries. I don't remember any African countries, though. My school wasn't that progressive. We also had fun Halloween carnivals with games, prizes, and many homemade treats for the best homemade costumes. Summers in LA were the best. Mom always made sure that we had an ample supply of popsicles. Our household was a make-do household, so we usually made the popsicles ourselves in Rubbermaid popsicle molds, where we froze Kool-Aid sweetened with plenty of sugar. Summertime was also a time of swimming and skating. Since we didn't have a car, we walked everywhere. People knew Mom as the bicycle lady since she rode her bike to the market to pick up groceries. One instance that I always remember was when Mom returned home struggling with bags of groceries on her bicycle, and tied to her handlebar were three inflated balloons: red, yellow, and blue. In our excitement, she untied the balloons and handed them to me. Somehow, I missed grabbing the strings, and the balloons floated into the white puffy clouds. I felt so sorry for Mom, knowing that she peddled all those blocks, mindful that she could lose the balloons before making it home, only for me to miss the handover. It was like running a 440-track race and my teammate handing off the baton to me, only for me to miss the grab, making all our four members lose the race. People watched as our balloons became airborne. Our neighborhood friends didn't let me forget that mishap.

My sisters and I learned to swim at Harvard Pool, near our home. We'd walk to the pool with our friends, the Davis boys, Kirk and Darryl, whose family had come from New Orleans. They lived at the end of the street and were our best friends. They worked as towel boys at the pool and eventually became junior lifeguards. Kirk taught me how to dive. Kirk and I were close. He gave me gifts of chameleon lizards. I named each of them Lizzie, after me, a name that Kirk also affectionately called me. Skating was our other activity, but the Davises could be rough. Our best skating partner was Gwendolyn Hughes. Her parents were from Texas. She was the only girl in a household of five brothers. We'd skate from the early afternoon into the late evening. The warm summer LA nights were nothing to be afraid of then. In our neighborhood, most children lived with two married parents who had migrated from either Louisiana or Texas and bought homes with front and back lawns. Our family was the smallest, with three children. It was a community where the children would visit each other's homes freely.

The Davises were Catholic and attended the Catholic parish school, St. Bridget, right across the street from our school, Western Avenue Elementary School. Even though we attended Methodist church, my sisters and I often chose to go to St. Bridget with the Davis boys instead of Vermont Square Methodist Church with my mother. Mom didn't mind. Church was church. Daddy didn't go to church. We knew the Catholic liturgy because the Davis boys, who were also choirboys, taught us. They'd give us gifts of crosses, the Virgin Mary, and St. Christopher medals, and we'd wear them proudly. We almost took catechism lessons. We embraced into our Methodist church as we grew older and away from the Davis boys. But my oldest sister eventually formally adopted Catholicism and joined St. Bridget as an adult.

Swimming lessons, apricots from our backyard trees, and watermelons from the watermelon man's truck seemed to go hand in hand with summer in Los Angeles. "Watermelons, watermelons, come get your sweet, juicy, red watermelons," the watermelon man chimed as neighbors poured out of their screened front doors to join the line around his truck. According to my friends, our watermelon man had the sweetest melons in our village of transplants. My sisters and I thought so, too.

The watermelon man reminded me of my Uncle Joe, a bootblack on the side, who worked at the Goodyear rubber factory during the week. Uncle Joe wasn't a relative, but he and his wife, Aunt Helen, had no children, so my sisters and I filled that void. He'd pick us up from our home in his big white and turquoise blue Buick with head and taillights sticking out of the front and rear of the car like rockets and drive us south to San Pedro for barbecue. He wore a captain's hat like Count Basie and smelled of the stale cigar that always hung out of his mouth, stuck between his dark lips. But my most vivid image of him was his fat fingers with black shoe polish in the cracks. He was very easygoing and unafraid to exhibit his Southern upbringing. Like many others, he and Aunt Helen were good people who had also made the migration trek from East Texas. And we were always happy to see them. Plus, Aunt Helen had a gigantic fig tree in her yard. I loved to eat the figs as soon as I picked them, standing under the tree and marveling at its outstretched branches full of even more figs.

As summer ended, we knew fall had arrived because our sycamore tree told us so with its yellow and orange leaves. It was time to change our food rituals from popsicles and watermelon to popcorn and hot chocolate on the table waiting for us after school when we opened the front door to our house. The food treats added to how Mom made us feel secure in our little neighborhood. Sometimes, we opened the door to a bowl of cooked white rice with a dollop of butter. Other times, Mom, like her mother, served us bread for our snack. She also went whole country and baked a skillet of yellow cornbread. She put a big yellow wedge in our bowls and poured buttermilk over it, sprinkling sugar on the top. It may sound unappealing to some, but it was heavenly to us. Thanks to Clabber Girl Baking Powder, the cornbread arced three inches high at its center when baked in a ten-inch cast-iron skillet. Grandma used real clabber—a type of soured milk—from the dairy cow's milk in Shreveport, but in LA, Mom settled for Clabber Girl to get the desired height and taste. It wasn't the same as Grandma's, but it was close. Thinking about it now, all of Grandma's ingredients came from the farm: the ground corn from the field and the buttermilk, churned butter, and clabber from the cows. So yes, Mom was serving us Lakeside Dairy food.

The cool weather turned into winter, often cooler but not cold. More and more vegetable soups and beans, especially red beans, rice, and black-eyed peas, entered our meals. Mom made a big cast-iron pot of beans each week, which she served with a side of collard, turnip, or mustard greens and a wedge of cornbread. Pops, my father, always ate meat—sausage, beef, or pork chops—and crispy fried chicken topped with a reddish-orange southwest Louisiana hot sauce from New Iberia. The aromas from his meals filled our house and wafted out of our screened door into the neighborhood, where they mixed with other smells of Louisiana and Texas cuisine.

As modern girls, we looked forward to Saturday when we cooked with our mother any time of the year—Campbell's tomato soup from a can, grilled cheese or pimento cheese sandwiches, fish sticks, or our favorite, tacos. Mom frequently lavished us with a gigantic apple pie topped with melted cheddar cheese. Why cheese, I wondered. "My mother put cheese on her pie," said Mom. I later learned that it is more of a New England, Pennsylvania, and midwestern dairy-centric tradition and one practiced by other dairy-farming families. Her apple pies were also a favorite at our school festivals, where she shared her Granny Smith apple pie recipe in our school's Parents and Teachers Association cookbook. I liked mom's pie because of its sweet and tart combination, especially with a dollop of vanilla ice cream. The flavors were heavenly.

Then came the holidays. Ours were busy with our handmade craft projects. In autumn, each week, our sycamore tree sent waves of leaves that floated in the air and painted our green lawn and gray sidewalk brown. We raked leaves each weekend until the final droppings for the year were gone. As the few remaining brown sycamore leaves floated to the ground, we helped Mom gather some to arrange throughout the house and give her sisters to decorate their homes. Our teachers also knew about our tree and asked my mom to send leaves to school to share for our art projects. At school, we painted the warm colors of fall harvests—yellow, orange, and red—on the crisp brown leaves larger than my adult hands. We pinned them to the bulletin board of our classroom and in the hallway by the principal's office.

A December chill washed over us as we donned our sweaters from Sears and Roebuck, Co., yet the sun still cast a warming glow on everything as we made homemade holiday garlands of tree branches from our backyard lemon trees. Everyone in the neighborhood came to us for lemons. Mothers sent their children to our door, "Mrs. LeFalle, can we have some lemons," they'd say. Mom was very generous, even when kids showed up at our door asking, "Mrs. LeFalle, can we have a cup of sugar and two eggs?" So, we decorated our home with homemade holiday garlands made of lemon tree branches. Bowls full of lemons filled our house with aromas of citrus, much to Mom's delight, competing with and often overpowering Pop's cigarette smoke.

With so many lemons, Mom took the same approach with apricots: waste nothing. Before the modern trend of seasoning with lemon juice, mom squeezed lemon juice on just about everything she boiled, baked, and sautéed. She made a new batch of lemonade every week, and once or twice a month, she baked Pops a lemon meringue pie, his favorite. The meringue stood about three inches high, like her cornbread, and the filling was an inch to inch-and-a-half. Her pies had meringue peaks with hints of light brown. They reminded me of a mountain range. They were soft and tasted divine. Unfortunately, my eczema kept me from enjoying lemonade, but Mom cut lemon wedges for my hot tea. And even better than the lemon meringue pie, I liked her zesty fresh lemon pound cake, which I could eat with joy and glee.

Our public elementary school held Christmas celebrations. We sang Christmas carols in school and church. I still love the hymns that we used to sing, and although it never snowed in LA, during the Christmas season, Mom would prepare everything as if we were living in a cold, farm-like winter. The greenery, cookies, decorations, carols, and delightful shopping trips by city bus to downtown LA to see the animated displays in department store windows were all seasonal rituals.

Mom was again on call at Christmas to supply our classes with holiday décor. But, instead of shiny, sparkly decorations, she brought Christmas greens of leafy lemon tree branches in place of the bunches of holly with red berries and pinecones that she often gathered in Louisiana for her mom. One year, my class performed "'Twas the Night Before Christmas." Mom's task was to make the antlers for the nine tiny reindeer. We helped Mom prop the tall ladder under our barren sycamore tree while we held it in place. She climbed up with a pair of loppers to prune enough branches to make eight sets of antlers and one more set for Rudolph. Finally, for the play, she fastened them to the heads of our schoolmates with a red ribbon.

Our teachers didn't expect such creative problem-solving from Black women, especially from the South. But the one Black teacher did, having come from a progressive Southern family, too, that had to be creative in the poorly funded schools of her Southern hometown. She smiled one of those coded inside smiles of approval to my mom. She needed no words to express her appreciation, and Mom responded to her with a nod and smile, acknowledging her thanks.

On Christmas Day, Mom reminded everyone that it was my birthday and that the Catholic nuns at Queen of Angels Hospital, where I was born, walked down the delivery room halls singing Christmas carols to celebrate Jesus's birth. I liked to think they sang for me, too, because Mother said I was a unique child born on Christmas Day, which I believed was true. But my most vivid memory of when the weather turned cold was eating yogurt. We ate it most of the year to stave off seasonal illnesses, especially during the fall and winter. Later in life, I learned of the immune-boosting properties of unsweetened plain yogurt, which is where my seasonal story began, with Mom and her life on her parent's Lakeside Dairy farm. Her dairy memories were woven into my growing up in LA. I've reflected on them at different points in my life, and their consoling images appear in my thoughts. Mom was an "earth mother" before I knew what it was. Her dairy memories were part of growing up in my family. She had us working in our planted beds, cleaning the succulents, transplanting, and deadheading their stalks of spent flowers because of her connection to the earth. She was born on a dairy, in an upstairs bedroom of a two-story farmhouse in northern Louisiana, where the air, scented with cow manure and milk, wafted into the up-drawn sash windows and through the billowing cotton curtains. She was familiar with the sounds and smells of the rural lands around her. On the farm, she drank the milk and ate the yogurt from the cows in the large dairy barn at the end of a well-worn path from the back of the house. Although she didn't make yogurt, it was part of our diet as it was for her. Her commitment to sustaining that part of life on that dairy farm and its fertile pastures was why I was on my knees in Mom's LA garden of succulents that surrounded our home in a community of other Louisianans. Remembering my upbringing and hers is how I got to this place to write about my grandparents' dairy. It connects me with Mom's actions and centers on food, especially yogurt.

In an ever-sprawling Los Angeles, those elementary school years were wonderfully cohesive—something that all children should experience— the feeling of being wanted and loved by friends and family and

Lizzetta LeFalle and Mom after high school.

safe and sheltered from the outside world. For my sisters and me, LA was simple and uncomplicated.

After graduating high school mid-year, I went to a local community college to beef up on some classes, and that's where I met Judy Saguchi; both of us enrolled in color, design, and drawing classes. Oswaldo was also in our class, and when the section had ended, Judy asked if we would join her on a cross-country trip. I wanted to ride the train across the country. But a drive across the country with her along Route 66 sounded like the adventure I needed. The only thing was that all three of us would be traveling in her tiny Karmann Ghia, and Oswaldo was over six feet tall!

Judy invited Oswaldo to have a man with us, and he almost didn't make it because of his mother. All of us still lived with our parents. While my mother was hesitant, Oswaldo's mother was downright suspicious—she was from Spain. She wanted us to know he was Spanish, not Mexican, or from another Hispanic culture who immigrated to Los Angeles. I can only imagine her distrust of me, a young Black girl, and Judy, who was Japanese. He was soft-spoken, but we could tell that he wanted in—he was desperate to get out from under the control of his mother, who, it seemed, wanted to clip his wings for life. I can't remember if his father lived with them, for I only saw her, and she was not friendly to Judy and me for placing ideas in her son's head about leaving her to travel across the country in a sports car—did I say he was over six feet tall?

That summer, Judy, Oswaldo, and I struck out on Route 66 for Chicago, where her uncle taught medicine at Northwestern University in Evanston, Illinois. Judy had planned the trip, and Oswaldo and I were her traveling partners. It was not my planned train ride across the country. Nevertheless, it was my opportunity to see the landscape very low to the ground. Daddy used to hum Nat King Cole's rendition of Route 66, and the words stuck out in my head as a great adventure. It was in 1967—the midst of the civil rights and Black Nationalism movements. We didn't realize the real pulse of the country until we got on the road and began driving into the Texas panhandle and Oklahoma. Men in pick-up trucks with hunting rifles on racks in the back cabs of their trucks pulled up next to us. They peered into Judy's Karmann Ghia that almost touched the ground—were we Freedom Riders? One sheriff thought so when he stopped us in a small town one night, and he said so. "I thought y'all was some of those Freedom Riders," he said as he peered inside our car and waived us on. Of course, it didn't help that we had California plates. But we made it to and from Chicago—the great adventure of our youth. Even though it was fun, I was happy to be headed back west, thinking of Nat all the way and mouthing the words, "If you ever plan to motor west, Travel my way, Take the highway that's the best, Get your kicks on Route 66."

In the fall, I went to the University of California, Santa Barbara, just two hours away. It was the life-altering distance I needed from my insular Black central LA community. College life is supposed to broaden one intellectually and socially. It presented opportunities for experimentation and exploring areas of my identity confined to the twenty square blocks of my Los Angeles community. The road trip with Judy and Oswaldo was a signal of things to come. At university, among other art and dance students, I skinny dipped in a mountain creek by moonlight, taught kids batik dyeing and candle making at a summer camp on a beach, and choreographed and performed modern dances.

Even then, I was into self-development, applying for a Behavioral Studies Research project in the summer of 1969 at the University of

California, Davis, in Northern California. I drove my 1965 Bahamas Blue VW with a yellow and green sunflower plastered onto the back hood up to Davis, where we lived in a communal setting and talked about social issues and politics. Davis was where I learned how to use a welding torch to fascine junk metal together to form sculptures. My mother gladly accepted my sculptures as junk art. They remained in her backyard until she moved into Aunt Lilly's empty flat in San Francisco in the early 1990s.

Davis was hot as hell, and after our sessions, we'd retreat to the pool, where we played water polo. We regularly visited alternative living situations throughout San Francisco's North and South Bay Areas in Santa Cruz. We stayed at communes with many lost souls trying to figure out their lives, but who knew they wanted a different existence than their parents—and they were from all over. In the mid to late 1960s, the San Francisco Bay Area was a mecca for youth and alternative perspectives on life.

The Davis experience, combined with already having to strip nude as a dancer to change costumes in the wings of theaters with male dancers, made me even more comfortable with my body. As an uninhibited visual artist in graduate school, I took a job modeling nude for a former instructor's painting and drawing classes. His blonde-haired wife was also an artist, and I taught courses at the junior college. We alternated modeling for classes at the continuing education program at Santa Barbara Community College, a program I later taught for six years.

Santa Barbara had gotten too hot for the revolutionary Black brothas, so they packed up and headed for the hills with other White alternatives to Mount Shasta, California. My boyfriend and I were on the tail end of our relationship, and he was transferring to Reed College in Portland, Oregon. As an experienced road traveler, I rode with him and the group. After dropping off the brothas in Mount Shasta, we headed for Portland. I said goodbye to my boyfriend. It was the last time I saw him. I took a bus or train to Seattle at the end of July. I caught a taxi to Aunt Alice's house in the Washington Heights neighborhood of Seattle. It was a three-story Victorian house on a corner where Aunt Alice and Uncle Linzy lived with their grandson, also named Linzy, and her grandchildren Matthew and Michelle, whose mother, Merle, passed suddenly of an aneurysm. Their father, Earl, was a career serviceman I met once while I was there during my month's stay.

Aunt Alice Bates Burton Macklin.

Aunt Alice, a dressmaker and designer, was so happy to see me because few of her family had moved to the far north of the Pacific Northwest in those days. I fondly remember her Sunday dinners, where she'd pull out all the stops. She collected antiques and antique dishes, donned the table with sparkling fluted glasses, and painted Italian, French, and English bowls, plates, and cups. I know because I turned everyone upside down to see their markings. It was dizzying to see Aunt Alice at work in the kitchen. It was "Sunday dinner," and the big meal had to feed us and our other relatives living in Seattle. The following Saturday evening, Aunt Alice asked me what I planned to make for Sunday dinner. I hadn't intended to make anything, but she welcomed me into her home like I had always been there. She said that's what her mother would have done.

I was an extra mouth, and because of that, I decided to make rice pudding. I didn't know how to cook many things, but my mother used to make rice pudding with leftover rice, and luckily, we had a bowl left over from Saturday's dinner. Because we ate beans once or twice a week, my mother cooked large pots of long-grain white rice. We were a rice-eating family; rather than potato-eating, we always had ample amounts of cooked rice. It was a side dish with gravy or butter. But sometimes, Mom made an extra amount of rice for rice pudding. We loved it with raisins, and it is so simple to make. I decided to rise early, before breakfast, to get myself together. By the time other family members came stumbling into the kitchen, I already had my ingredients, simple as they were, mixed and ready for the oven. So, I made that for dessert. I had never made it for anyone but myself, but as the old folks say, I put my foot in this one this time.

Aunt Alice loved it when my mother took the train ride up to Seattle, and now her niece made the trip. She took me to yardage shops, and we sewed together that gray and rainy month. I continued to cook dishes from my limited culinary repertoire to a very appreciative Aunt Alice. Recently, I asked Cousin Michelle about Aunt Alice.

"She was indeed a designer. She designed and made dresses, evening gowns, bridal gowns, and men's suits too. She was able to make garments just by seeing them in magazines, catalogs, etc. Later in life, she made most of my mother's clothes and many of my clothes when I was a child. She also made costumes for the Seattle Opera and local theater companies."

—COUSIN MICHELLE FLOWERS-TAYLOR

While in Seattle, it rained every day except for two days. With all the rain, I longed for sunshine and warmth, which I returned to at summer's end. Aunt Alice was one of my mother's older sisters, and unfortunately, I only saw her once more after that visit. But, upon reflection, staying with Aunt Alice completed my circle of knowing and communing with my mother's Louisiana siblings, who decided to travel west. They had come to the end of the country and could not go any further by land. Daddy's Red Cap job encouraged my curiosity about traveling. I continued to travel in planes to Europe, Africa, the Caribbean, and South and North America, still thinking of his train rides while riding the road.

Yellow Cornmeal Cornbread.

YELLOW CORNMEAL CORNBREAD

"Bread and butter come to supper.
If you're late, you won't get nothing."
—MOM

I remember the aroma of Mom's cornbread luring us into the kitchen from play. We could hardly wait until the bread came out of the oven— we wanted it hot and steamy. So, she obliged us, even though she made it to go with a "mess o' greens" or beans.

I don't know the source of the rhyme that Mom used to call my sisters and me to come to the table and eat. But, yes, my mother thought it improper to eat anywhere other than the table, even if it was only for a snack of cornbread and buttermilk.

Hands-on time: 25 minutes
Total time: 35 minutes
Serves: 6–8

Ingredients:
  1 ¼ cup yellow cornmeal
  1 ¼ cup all-purpose flour
  2 tsp. baking powder
  1 tsp. salt
  1 tsp. baking soda
  granulated sugar
  ⅔ cup canola oil, melted unsalted butter, or bacon fat (1/3 in the
    batter, ⅓ for the skillet)
  2 cups buttermilk
  2 Tbsp. salted butter, melted, to top cornbread after baking
  2 eggs

Preparation:
  Preheat the oven to 400°F. Mix yellow cornmeal, flour, baking pow-der, salt, and sugar in a dry bowl. In another bowl, combine oil, eggs, and buttermilk. Fold wet ingredients into dry. Heat remaining canola oil, unsalted butter, or bacon fat in an 8-inch cast-iron skillet. When the oil is hot, pour the batter mixture into the skillet. It will sizzle for a few minutes, making the edges crisp. Turn off the flame and immediately place the skillet into the oven. Bake for approximately 25 minutes or until a knife stuck into the center comes out clean but not dry. If the blade is wet, return the cornbread to the oven for a few additional minutes. Liberally butter the top of the bread with salted butter.

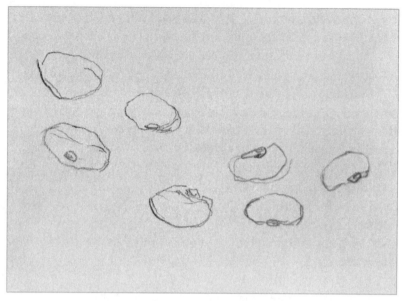

Red Beans. Illustration by author.

RED BEANS AND RICE

Louis Armstrong often signed off his musical engagements and letters "Am Red Beans and Ricely Yours" because it was one of his favorite meals.[1] As a "red beans and ricely" family, we ate the savory beans at least once a week. On the weekend, my father got up early to put the large cast-iron Dutch oven pot of his beans on the gas flame of our kitchen range. It cooked for hours as he watched the television or sat on our front porch swing and greeted neighbors. He was a cigarette smoker, and my mother preferred him to smoke outside as much as possible. We had a large backyard, but he liked sitting in the front of the house to watch over the neighborhood. He cooked enough beans to serve several meals with white rice throughout the week. My mother always baked a large skillet of cornbread to accompany the meal.

Hands-on time: 25 minutes
Total time: 3 hours
Serves: 8

Ingredients:

1 ½ cup small red beans

1 tsp. baking soda

1 Tbsp. unsalted butter

1 Tbsp. olive oil

1 cup diced medium yellow or brown onion

1 cup diced celery

1 cup diced bell pepper

3 cloves garlic, chopped

1 quart chicken stock (or veggie stock)

1 ham hock, optional

1 tsp. onion powder

1 tsp. garlic powder

1 tsp. dried thyme

1 tsp. paprika

2 Tbsp. black pepper

2 bay leaves

salt to taste

5 Tbsp. olive, butter, or other oil

diced tomato, for serving

Preparation:

Rinse and drain red beans. In this no-soak method, boil 4 quarts of water and add the beans. Once boiling, add baking soda. Boil beans for 1 minute. Drain, rinse, and bring beans to a boil again with ham hock and 2 quarts of water. In a separate pan, sauté onion, celery, bell pepper, and garlic in olive oil, butter, or other oil. Add minced ingredients to the bean pot. Mix in dry seasonings and bay leaves. Continue to boil beans for 2 hours, adding chicken stock as needed to prevent beans from sticking. I use chicken stock or bone broth to get a richer and healthier broth—test beans for tenderness and mash ¼ of the beans with a potato masher. Reduce heat to low and simmer for another hour. Continue cooking to your preferred consistency, add salt to taste, and top with tomatoes. I also shake a few drops of hot sauce and splash vinegar into my beans to brighten the taste. My mother added vinegar to most of her pots of greens and beans. Serve over long-grain white rice.

Granny Smith Apple. Illustration by author.

GRANNY SMITH APPLE PIE

I like the sweetness and tartness of my mom's Parent and Teachers Association (PTA) award-winning Granny Smith apple pie. This recipe is based on my mother's pie, but it isn't her exact recipe. Like most of her sisters, she did not write her recipes down. She followed the ingredients and tastes of her mother. So, I've turned to several Black cooks I respect and love and woven together my memories with their ingredients. Serve this pie with a scoop of vanilla ice cream for a heavenly treat.

Hands-on time: 15 minutes
Total time: 1 hour
Serves: 8

Ingredients:
6 cups sliced and peeled Granny Smith or Pippin apples
1 Tbsp. lemon juice
½ cup granulated sugar
½ cup brown sugar
¼ cup all-purpose flour
¼ tsp. ground nutmeg
½ tsp. ground cinnamon
pinch of salt
⅓ cup cut butter
2 tsp. vanilla
Trader Joe's or Whole Foods frozen pie crusts (If you want to make
   it yourself, I suggest Martha Stewart's basic pie crust.)

Preparation:
Preheat oven to 425°F. Prepare one unbaked pie crust by rolling
and fitting it into a 9-inch pie plate. In a large bowl, squeeze lemon
juice over the apples and toss to prevent browning. Add sugar, flour,
nutmeg, cinnamon, and salt to the apples and toss to combine well.
Pour apple mixture into the prepared pie crust. Cut butter into small
pieces and place over the top of the apple mixture. Roll out the second unbaked pie crust and center it over the top of the pie. Seal the
top and bottom crusts together around the edges. Sprinkle the top
of the pie with additional sugar, if desired. Cut slits into the top of
the pie to allow the steam to escape while cooking. Bake for 40 to
50 minutes until the pie bubbles and the crust is golden brown. If
desired, brush the top crust with melted salted butter during the
last 10 minutes of baking. If it browns too fast, protect the pie crusts
with strips of aluminum foil to prevent them from over-browning.
Allow the pie to cool completely before slicing. Serve with vanilla
ice cream or whipped cream.

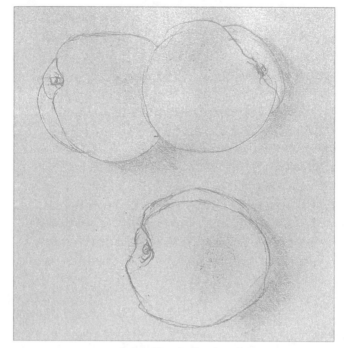

Apricots. Illustration by author.

STEWED APRICOTS WITH LEMON

We had so many apricots that Mom had to do something with them. She'd often stew them with lemons from our trees, but other times, she'd make apricot pies with the same flaky crust she used to make her beloved double-crusted apple pies. I've often found that some pie and cobbler makers create their desserts too sweet for my tastes. I like a combination of sweet and tart, the taste sensation I get when biting into a fresh peach, plum, or apricot.

Preparation:
   Wash, halve, and pit 5 to 6 pounds of fresh apricots. Cut out any hard parts around the pit. Cut apricots in quarters or smaller depending on the size of the apricots. Put in a pan with ¼ cup of water. Sprinkle in sugar and lemon slices and cook over medium heat, stirring so the apricots do not stick to the pan. Add water as needed. If you have a lot of apricots, you can wash, pit, and blanch them before freezing them.

Fresh Lemon. Illustration by author.

FRESH LEMON BUTTER POUND CAKE

This soft, fresh lemon pound cake tastes like those old-fashioned pound cakes that folks sent as gifts from their kitchens in the South to family members who had migrated far away from their homes. The tastes were reminders of their joyous times with their now-distant families. Those Southern communities of lack folks joined at each other's homes to create communities through storytelling and food.

Hands-on time: 20 minutes
Total time: 1 hour, 40 minutes
Serves: 10–12

Ingredients:
    1 cup unsalted butter, softened
    3 cups granulated sugar
    6 large eggs, separated
    ⅓ cup plus 2 Tbsp. fresh lemon juice, divided
    ⅓ cup grated lemon zest
    3 cups all-purpose flour, sifted
    ¼ tsp. salt

¼ tsp. baking soda
1 cup plus 2 tsp. whole milk, divided
2 cups confectioners' sugar

Preparation:

Preheat oven to 325°F. Grease a 12- to 15-cup loaf pan with melted butter and dust with flour. In a stand mixer bowl, beat butter and granulated sugar at medium speed until fluffy (or thoroughly mix by hand until well combined and smooth). Add egg yolks, one at a time, beating well after each addition. Add 1/3 cup fresh lemon juice and half the lemon zest. Whisk together flour, salt, and baking soda in a medium bowl. Gradually add flour mixture to butter mixture alternating with 1 cup milk, beginning and ending with flour mixture, beating until just combined after each addition. Beat egg whites with a mixer at high speed in a medium bowl until stiff. Fold into batter. Pour batter into the prepared pan. Bake until a wooden pick inserted near the center comes out clean, 1 hour and 10 minutes to 1 hour and 15 minutes. Let cool in the pan for 10 minutes. Remove from pan and let cool entirely on a wire rack. Whisk together the remaining 2 Tbsp. lemon juice, lemon zest, and 2 Tbsp. milk in a medium bowl. Gradually whisk in the confectioner's sugar until smooth. Drizzle over the cake.

Chapter One

THE BATES SIBLINGS FIND A HOME IN LOS ANGELES

WE PICKED LEMONS, APRICOTS, BLACKBERRIES, CONCORD AND GREEN grapes, and rhubarb stalks in our backyard. Oranges and apples came from the market. Mrs. Helen brought us black-eyed peas and collard greens from Watts. We gave her lemons from our trees. Aunt Lizzetta grew watermelons in her backyard among her giant agave plants. Aunt Phoebe made cherry brandy. Uncle Angus went to Baton Rouge and Shreveport to catch shrimp and catfish. He was the gumbo master of the family. When we visited Aunt Lilly in San Francisco, we always had baked Cornish hens and that San Francisco treat, chicken-flavored Rice-A-Roni, with her added sprinkling of paprika.

My family came from Shreveport in two waves: the 1920s to the late 1930s and the 1940s and 1950s. They followed other Louisiana families migrating mainly from metropolitan centers in the state. A community of Blacks settled in mid-city Los Angeles before World War II and the great exodus of Blacks out of the South. Their numbers were fewer and more affluent. Aunt Lena and her brother Leonard Bates, the children from my grandpa's first marriage, settled in Los Angeles in 1925. They were too early for defense-related industries and other federal jobs in southern Los Angeles. They worked and serviced Hollywood's primary industry, entertainment. Uncle Leonard initially lived with Grandma with his wife and infant child at the dairy home, but when the infant died, he left and came to Los Angeles. He worked as a porter for a hotel. In Los Angeles, Aunt Lena worked as a cleaner in an apartment building. When her husband, the chauffeur Bennie Morris, died five years after they arrived in LA, she had to fend for herself. She went into service

Young Aunt Lena at the dairy barn.

work for several Hollywood-connected families living in Beverly Hills. Aunt Lena embraced the look of Hollywood actresses, donning their makeup styles. It was a cross between the Mae West and Bette Davis looks. It was scary to me. Much later, my older cousin explained the origins of her look. I understood better why she looked the way she did.

> "In the 1930s, Lena worked for Mae West."
> —COUSIN MICHAEL [UNCLE BOOKER T'S SON]

Black women with Aunt Lena's phenotype, with very fair skin and a head full of wavy hair, were often encouraged to audition for small parts in Hollywood films. Some women were also available for clandestine activities. Aunt Lena frequented the Dunbar Hotel, where the Pullman porters stayed on their stops in LA. Most Pullman porters were Black when the migration began, and it continued to be a profession for Black men until the 1950s. One well-known formerly enslaved

Pullman employee, Rufus Estes, a chef, signed on with the Pullman Company at age twenty-six to cook for his luxury rail cars. While working in Chicago in 1911, Estes penned *Good Things to Eat, as Suggested by Rufus*, considered one of the first cookbooks by a professional Black chef. Soon after, he moved to Los Angeles, a place he had visited as a Pullman employee, to escape the midwestern winters. From the 1920s until he died in 1938, he lived and worked as a chef in LA.[1]

Initially, the early porters lived at The American Hotel, which opened in 1905 as a small, well-furnished hotel for Black travelers at the end of the rail line. After enslavement, Pullman hired many freed Blacks with hospitality skills, including maids, chefs, and waiters. Although often demeaned by the White passengers, their Pullman jobs translated to propelling them into the Black middle class.

In 1928, Drs. John and Vada Somerville built the Hotel Somerville on Central Avenue in Los Angeles. There, Black travelers could stay in style and comfort during the era when restrictive laws on segregation banned Black people from major hotels. The hotels even barred well-known entertainers like Louis Armstrong, Ella Fitzgerald, Lena Horne, and Billie Holiday. The Somervilles sold the hotel after the stock market crash in 1929, and the new owners named it The Dunbar, honoring poet Paul Laurence Dunbar.[2] The Dunbar also became the epicenter of the Los Angeles jazz scene in the 1940s and 1950s.[3]

Aunt Lula and her husband, Uncle "Private Carter" David, went to New York before coming to Los Angeles in 1932. I don't know what he did in Los Angeles, but he probably worked club scenes as he had in New York. Aunt Lula became a domestic worker, mainly cooking and preparing meals and delicacies for wealthy Whites and Blacks for garden parties. Their father did not let his daughters do that kind of work at home.

"He didn't let the sisters work for White families. He was very protective of the sisters and didn't want to risk the Whites trying to bed with them."

—UNCLE ANGUS

My mother and sisters called Aunt Lula's husband Private Carter because he served in the army. We knew him as Uncle Sonny. He left Shreveport and lived in New York before settling in LA and working in similar club scenes. Since Central Avenue was already a social mecca for Blacks, especially for performers with ties to Hollywood, it became the center of culture for Black art production and expression.[4] Jazz music and its musicians blossomed on Central Avenue. In the 1940s, West Coast jazz was born in the Central Avenue District due to the influx of musicians from New Orleans into LA and the formation of social dance bands. New York musicians took note and brought the sounds of bebop to LA.[5] Black musicians like Lena Horne, Louis Armstrong, and Ella Fitzgerald performed in films and when in LA, at Black clubs on Central Avenue. The clubs drew integrated and international audiences. Even Langston Hughes came to Los Angeles and wrote for Hollywood. Black performances in film, concerts, and live theater spilled into Black churches and shows for Black social clubs and schools.

Aunt Lizzetta joined Aunt Lena and Aunt Lula in Los Angeles in 1937, two years after their father died in 1935. Although Aunt Lizzetta did not want to leave the family home, she and her husband, Clement, had just lost their first child, Clement Jr., in a tragic accident. He was only eight days old. While sleeping, Aunt Lizzetta rolled over onto him, smothering the baby. She was devastated and could not fathom what she had done. She and Clement moved to Los Angeles, but the thought of the tragedy lingered with her. She embraced her life in Los Angeles and worked at the Ye Olde Waffle Shoppe on Central Avenue with her friend, Margaret, another native from Shreveport. It was popular, and Black Hollywood celebrities and visiting musicians frequented it and left generous tips. Aunt Lizzetta and Lena purchased homes, and they were the first places to land until their siblings got jobs to rent their apartments or buy their homes. They co-signed mortgage papers and loaned cash to family members. Family members came and went. This practice continued for subsequent generations. Their parents ingrained homeownership in their children, striving to improve their social struc-ture in their Allendale community in Shreveport. As a result, all the Bates siblings in California, except Uncle Booker, accomplished the dream of homeownership. Before World War II, more Black residents owned homes in Los Angeles than any other major city.[6]

My mother came to Los Angeles after the war started in the 1940s. She completed one year at Southern University in Baton Rouge, majoring in physical education, but the math requirement, with her other classes, made it too difficult to continue. Then, she moved to Philadelphia to

Aunt Mabel in Philadelphia.

live with one of her oldest sisters, Mabel. Grandma taught her how to sew, so Mom enrolled in tailoring school, which she liked and did well.

However, life in Philadelphia's overcrowded Black neighborhoods was not for her either. She wanted a home life like in Shreveport and decided to join five of her siblings in Los Angeles. In LA, she also resumed her tailoring studies at Frank Wiggin's (now Trade Technical College) Tailoring School to fine-tune her tailoring skills. After graduating, a Beverly Hills fashion house hired her for hand needlework; she had ample work as a tailor because of the film industry.

She remembers Aunt Lena dressing up to look like Mae West during her first year in Los Angeles. One night, Aunt Lena did not return home. Instead, she spent the night with Steve Springer, a friend from Shreveport, at The Dunbar Hotel, where the Pullman railroad porters stayed overnight. That night, police raided the hotel, and she was arrested for prostitution, although Aunt Lena maintained that was not the case. He was just a friend she and her sisters knew from Shreveport. As a result, she was not charged and released.

Aunt Lena later married Uncle Bill Day, a Pullman porter for the railroad. The terminus for his train out of New Orleans was Los Angeles's Union Station. He stayed at The Dunbar, where he probably met Aunt Lena. Uncle Bill was a tall, thin, brown-skinned, and quiet-spoken man. Aunt Lena wanted more money to resume the type of life she had lived with Bennie. Marrying Uncle Bill meant Aunt Lena no longer had to work in service. She continued to work by getting side work in the Hollywood entertainment community. Like most other Blacks coming to LA, Aunt Lena and Uncle Bill first settled east of Broadway on the east side of Los Angeles around Central Avenue before moving westward. The White covenants did not restrict Blacks to homeownership on the east side but deterred their dreams of owning properties in other parts of LA. When the covenants lifted, she moved west.

Aunt Lena and Uncle Bill bought a lot at Jefferson and 10th Avenue, hired a Black builder, and built a house from the ground. She painted it bright pink, and Cousin Michael remembers seeing her wearing overalls as she wielded her hammer and worked alongside the builder. Uncle Bill was still working for the railroad. Then, when the covenants that barred Blacks from moving into Leimert Park were lifted, Aunt Lena and Uncle Bill bought a home on Sutro Avenue there, where they lived until he died. Then, alone again, she sold the house and moved to an apartment in the Baldwin Hills Jungle, named for its profusion of tropical landscaping.

When Aunt Lena married Uncle Bill, Mom lived with Aunt Lizzetta. She got Mom a café job to work alongside her at Ye Ole Waffle Shoppe. Aunt Lena worked at the café too. Aunt Lizzetta married Uncle Willie Moore, another former serviceman, and she and her friend Margaret also decided to play matchmakers and introduce my father to my mother. Dad was recently out of the army as a chaplain's assistant, and they thought Mom and Dad would make a good match. After they married, then came the babies. My older sister and parents lived in an apartment building near Aunt Lizzetta. When I was born, my mother named me Lizzetta, honoring the sister who had helped her in multiple ways in her new city of LA.

Calling me by the same name also meant she shared me with her sister, who had lost her son. I didn't learn about the tragedy of Aunt Lizzetta's baby for many years. But when I did, I understood why Aunt Lizzetta cared about my two sisters and me. I gravitated toward her,

Lizzetta LeFalle as a toddler, LA.

Mom and Aunt Lizzetta at her home in LA.

not understanding the full story of her loss, but I knew that I was very dear to her. Aunt Lizzetta invited us to move into her house, and we lived there until my mother was ready to give birth to her third child.

The money my parents saved by living with Aunt Lizzetta helped them place a down payment on our house in a neighborhood rapidly changing from White to Black. It was something that families did in those days, supporting each who made the journey to the coast. When my family settled in Los Angeles—west of Hoover, north of Gage, south of Adams, and east of Crenshaw—the area became our village. For many years, Los Angeles was governed by de facto segregation and racial restrictions maintained through redlining. People of color could only purchase homes in the regions that did not have White-only covenants, mainly on the east side of LA.

Before the Great Migration of Blacks west to California, a few well-established Black families lived in major West Coast cities. Many Black people were limited to service jobs catering to the wealthy. However, large numbers of Blacks taking advantage of the job openings in the aerospace industry and other defense-related industries frightened Whites, who felt Blacks competed with them for their jobs. They also feared Blacks moving into their neighborhoods.[7]

"All the Blacks had to live on the east side, not west of Broadway. If you were fair-skinned, you could get a job at May Co or Bullocks in the powder room or elevator. Black men couldn't get employment until Roosevelt signed the Executive Order [1941] declaration to outlaw racial discrimination in federal agencies. Before that, Black men would go downtown and collect old magazines from White people and sell them door to door to Whites and Blacks. They also went door to door, asking to do lawns, wash cars, etc."

—COUSIN MICHAEL

Hollywood also had a significant impact on LA Blacks. Even with full-time jobs, many had side hustles working in the entertainment industry, such as cooks, house cleaners, drivers, chauffeurs, and butlers to wealthy producers, directors, and writers. Some worked in "human extra" roles in films. My mother, father, and Aunt Lena all had "human extra" roles in Hollywood films. Mother played an extra in a scene in Billy Pastor's Café in the 1954 movie *Carmen Jones*, starring Harry Belafonte and Dorothy Dandridge singing "Dat's Love." Dad was in the 1952 landmark film about the Haitian Revolution, *Lydia Bailey*. He wore a straw hat while holding a horse, with eyes acknowledging the drumbeats of a simmering rebellion in the distance. Blacks sought after these minor roles for the extra cash they offered. My mom credited their family friend, Chester Jones, the consummate Hollywood Black character actor, for funneling her family members and friends into those minor roles. He had minimal film-speaking roles and was largely uncredited, even for speaking ones. But a paycheck allowed many Blacks to get a taste for that primary industry in Los Angeles. Jones worked in Hollywood in twenty-five films from 1941 until he died in 1975. I remember thumbing through my Aunt Lizzetta's photo albums and

Chester Jones in *A Streetcar Named Desire*.

finding a color picture of Chester as a vegetable street vendor in New Orleans's French Quarter in the 1951 film *A Streetcar Named Desire*.

Aunt Lizzetta and Lula worked for two prominent Jewish families in Beverly Hills, the B's and the K's, but Aunt Lizzetta also worked for executives at Capitol Records. She'd bring us the discarded copies of promotional albums. Most of them were recording sessions by folk singers like the Kingston Trio. Those albums introduced me to the current folk singers of the day. They nurtured my life-long appreciation for acoustic guitar strumming by Bob Dylan, Joan Baez, Peter, Paul and Mary, Richie Havens, and many more. In college, I purchased a guitar and, with the help of a friend from New York, taught myself to play some of the melodies I first heard on those albums and more.

My Aunts were very present in my life, especially Aunts Lilly and Lizzetta.

Aunt Lilly and Aunt Lizzetta, Los Angeles, 1954.

I still remember the late 1960s. One summer, Aunt Lula asked me to assist her with a garden brunch at one of her wealthy employer's homes. My world had expanded, and I was aware of Black folks' hardships during and after enslavement and the remaining oppressive measures used to keep Black people in mental bondage. But Mom always spoke of Aunt Lula's gift for creating inviting and delicious dishes for garden parties.

"She was best at preparing and serving garden parties. And she would fix a dainty lunch for me every Sunday after church, the same way she made them in service."

—MOM

Aunt Lula always invited my sisters and me to her home for tea parties. She'd dress a little round table with a frilly tablecloth, antique teacups, and plates. The silverware was silver! Mom insisted that we wear one of our finer dresses to attend our party. This memory came to me when Aunt Lula asked for my help. She was my soft-spoken and endearing Aunt Lula, so I agreed to help and support her, serving with

Aunt Lula is at work in Beverly Hills, California.

her at one of the garden parties. As I returned to college, I considered it a poignant lesson about keeping family near. She was very proud of me. She wanted her Jewish employers to see me and know me as a college student. In the end, it was something that they celebrated with her. So, I returned to college, but a lot happened at home while I was away.

I suppose every family has at least one tragic figure. But in Los Angeles, we had several. First, Aunt Lula's son, our cousin Bobby, lost his way with drugs. He spent much of his young life incarcerated. But Aunt Lizzetta thought Bobby's problems began with his mother, Aunt Lula.

"See, [when] Bobby was born, his little feet were rolled up like a scroll. And every day Mama would take him to the Shriners Hospital [the first hospital erected in 1922 by Shriners International Fraternity to provide free healthcare services to children].

I imagine they cut his leg like all the way down and straightened his legs. He was walking perfectly straight. But now, if Mama had not taken him to the Shriners Hospital, he would have been walking like right over left, like this. But Lula, when she was carrying Bobby, she went up to the office where a friend of hers was working. And the old doctor was crippled, so at home she was mocking this old doctor the way he was walking. And this is how Bobby happened to come there crippled.

Lula called me to come there one day. She said, Lizzetta come over here, Bobby's on the floor and I can't get him up. Honey, Bobby was right there, and he died right there. He had died at home. The ambulance came to get him, but he was already dead. But he had carried us on a merry-go-round before he left here. And how many days has he come here? One day he come here, he was all dressed down. So, I went to run the water in the bathtub so he could take a bath. He was fully dressed. And when I got back in the room, he had just gone to sleep with all his clothes, and shoes and everything on."

—AUNT LIZZETTA

Bobby's condition took a toll on Aunt Lula, causing her to wash her hands incessantly. She could barely stand to hold money in her hands, fearful of germs, as she tried to keep her mind together. At the time, no one recognized the early onset of Alzheimer's disease, which made it difficult for Aunt Lula to deal with Bobby's addiction. Aunt Lizzetta tried multiple times to break Bobby from his drug addiction, even locking him in her closets. Bobby would plead for her to let him out, and when she finally did, he'd leave the house in search of more drugs. It was something that his mother nor Aunt Lizzetta could understand. They did not know how to help him, and he didn't ask for help. He never posed a threat to them. Instead, he was meek and loving. I found him the same way when I visited him in prison.

I often recall that small village of my youth. Most of my mother's family, who migrated from Shreveport, lived within walking distance of our home. In LA, Whites moved out, and Black people from Louisiana and East Texas moved in. Most came on the Southern Pacific's Sunset Route from Shreveport, New Orleans, Baton Rouge, Houston, Fort Worth, and San Antonio. Many of the arrivals were educated, with personal and life experiences as landowners, and with rich traditions in foodways, music, and religious practices. My family left a stronghold of the Ku Klux Klan and regular lynching of Black men. They were used to thriving in their segregated community in Caddo Parish.[8] As their LA neighborhoods transformed from White to Black into physical and cultural spaces, extended family and friends crafted their new Southern homes and continued to thrive. My family bought a California bunga-low, a single-story home with two bedrooms, one bathroom, and a front and back yard. A roof overhang jutted out from the façade, meeting two sentry-like pillars that broadened as they fanned onto either side of the porch. Developers repeated this style of the building across LA's sprawling footprint.

Many communities were carbon copies of others, except for the color of the residents' skin. Bigoted covenants made our continued westward movement impossible, but they were challenged by the 1948 *Shelley v. Kraemer* ruling that racial covenants were unlawful. It opened all-White blocks of Leimert Park for Black, Japanese, and Mexican American homeowners. Whites moved west, north, and south as they moved in. Those who migrated West before and during the war from a Southern state took jobs where they could. They felt lucky to get railroad, military, film industry, and the United States Post Office jobs. Blacks continued to work as domestic cooks, chauffeurs, house cleaners, and butlers in nonspeaking roles in Hollywood films. Opportunities also became available to work in the Black business district on Central Avenue, a center for Black entrepreneurship. The Negro City Directory of Black Los Angeles, California (1930–1932) lists over seventy-five Black-owned businesses on or near Central Avenue. The businesses included barber and beauty shops, dentists, grocers, insurance companies, dressmakers, pharmacies, bakeries, and real estate brokers.[9] Other men continued to work as Red Cap porters who carried train passengers' baggage. With the rise in air travel, many train porters transferred to airport Skycap Porter positions. After working in food service in the late 1940s and early 1950s, Uncle Angus also worked as a Skycap to send extra money home to Grandma.

"When I went to California, Mom's house was leaking back home. I had an account at Sears on Slauson and Vermont. I asked Sears if they could put a roof on my folk's house in Shreveport and charge

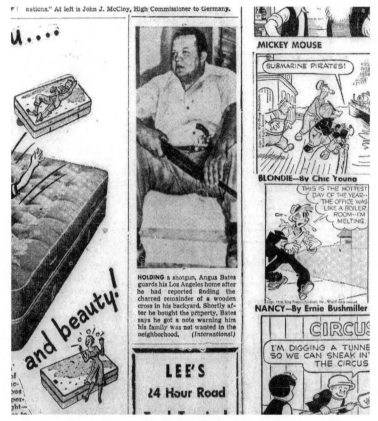

"One Man, Two-Gun Guard," Los Angeles in 1952.

it to the account. They did because I had an account—you can't do that these days. When the front and back porches were degrading, I told her to ask the Black carpenters to fix them, and I paid for it with the money I made in California. I sent my mother fifty dollars every Monday morning when I was at the airport—without fail. I sent her money to have the house fixed up. I paid to have the new windows, front and back porch. I made a hundred dollars a day at the airport, so it was no sweat."

—UNCLE ANGUS

Once employed, he married a woman he had known from New Orleans. They had a daughter, Angela, and settled in a home farther west from the family village, carved out by other Black LA transplants. One night, he awoke to "the charred remains of a wooden cross" in his manicured backyard. He was also warned that "he and his family were not wanted in the neighborhood." He moved too far west for some White folks. But whoever it was, they didn't know Uncle Angus. So, he resorted to sitting watch on his porch with a pistol and shotgun for three weeks, daring anyone to run him out of his new neighborhood. Uncle Angus eventually earned his teaching certification in chemistry and began teaching in the LA public schools. He later became a school principal. However, racist challenges continued to exist in Louisiana and California. Even as Uncle Angus continued to find employment in LA educational positions, he always maintained his relationships with sites in Louisiana. He also helped me to navigate New Orleans, where he frequently visited as a young man.

UNCLE'S WESTSIDE

Uncle moved into a White neighborhood
On the Westside of Los Angeles
Jumped out of bed one night
To see debris from a charred cross on his impeccably cut back
     lawn.
Being from Louisiana, he had grown up around White folks
His Papa's Papa was the White man across the pasture.
Uncle was from the old school.
He knew how to handle
This situation.
For three weeks
He sat on his porch with his pistol and hunting shotgun
Daring anyone else to challenge
His right to stay in his house
No one did.
No one was running him away from
His lovely new home on the Westside.
"I've come too far for that," said Uncle Angus.

—LIZZETTA LEFALLE-COLLINS

❀

DEATH'S FINGERS

I am in New Orleans, retracing the footsteps of Uncle Angus and his wife, Aunt Ursulina. I've traveled from northern to southern Louisiana, following my family's stories and my complex relationship with this place that holds visceral and familiar images for me. The New Orleans that Uncle Angus knew was where the dusky mornings squeezed the last blue hues out of the blue-black moonlit nights and where old oaks with mighty arms reached across streets to greet each other high up in the sky above Callé Esplanade. Like crooked, arthritic fingers, their limbs cast shadows in the darkness of the night, creating an eerie, death-like pall that swept up and down the street and sidewalks.

Uncle told me to be sure to visit the old neighborhood of Tremé just outside Le Vieux Carré, the French Quarter, one of the oldest Black communities in the nation and where he first met Aunt Ursulina. Both Tremé and the Quarter were awash in superstitions and beliefs embodied in the Catholic churches and the many alternative spirit houses that siphoned even the most devout Catholic away from the way of the cross into a realm steeped in animism. But human intermediaries whose discipline was to venerate the spirits guided both beliefs.

At the edge of Aunt Ursulina's neighborhood, I walked the old Quarter along the iron-gated buildings with trailing magenta bougainvillea plants. The buildings still had tile street signs dating back to Spain's occupation of New Orleans. When researching the city, I read about the Spanish galleons that traded coffee, gold, and silver bullion and enslaved Black people along the Atlantic and Caribbean coasts from Veracruz, Mexico, to Havana, Cuba, and back to the Port of New Orleans. Unfortunately, many ships ran aground in hurricane-infested seas or were bombarded by French and English vessels as they vied for their part of America, losing their bounty to an unforgiving sea that kept their secrets for hundreds of years, if not forever.

When I got to Tremé at Rue Saint Louis, I thought of her as I looked down the street lined with small clubs and cafes frequented mainly by Black residents. Across the street, I walked through the famed Saint Louis Cemetery, full of tombs dedicated to luminaries like voodoo priestess Marie Laveau. I felt Aunt Ursulina was with me as I roamed the maze of marble or whitewashed cement homes for the dead in this city of the spirits.

Aunt Ursulina was born into this neighborhood with too many bars and too much sorrow. She quickly became a ward of the old convent of the Ursuline Sisters. The Sisters still lived in the cloistered rooms two blocks from Rue Saint Louis in Le Vieux Carré. They named her after their convent. I went looking for the convent. I walked up and down streets, and there it was, in front of me. I couldn't see the full convent yard, only the roses on the iron fence. Walking farther to the corner of the gated yard led to the steps running to the street below.

Standing there, I caught a glimpse of the green layers of the garden—the white-slatted wooden structure in the style of an oversized Creole cottage dated back to the eighteenth century. In the springtime, a sculpture of the Blessed Virgin Mother, who stands among the lilies of the field, watches over the blooming garden and welcomes and forgives those of the parish that, in the heat of sexual passion, conceived babies that nobody cared for or wanted. Everyone knew they could bring them to the foot of the convent where the Ursuline Sisters, those earthly angels who cared for the poor, the needy, and the unwanted of the parish, received them.

The 1940s was an era of migration for many Southern Blacks to points elsewhere. Returning home to LA, I thought of Black Louisianans as they rolled into Los Angeles in high numbers, like distant waves from a Southern shore. Mom said Uncle Angus and Aunt Ursulina reconnected in LA as partying soul mates. They married and had a daughter, Angela. I never thought to ask Uncle if her name referred to "angel in LA," As they continued to drink, my mother, who already had two toddlers eighteen months apart and was pregnant with a third child, became Angela's unofficial guardian. Although not showing yet, in her state of motherhood, Mom was the nightly repository for Angela as her parents continued their quest for good times in this new city of overindulgence.

Our public school was across the street from Angela's Catholic school. Sometimes, we waved at each other from our respective playgrounds. I remember Aunt Ursulina dropping Angie, as we called her, off at our house after school with little conversation—she almost seemed nervously uncomfortable and vulnerable around my mother. Mom complained but accommodated her, seeing the sadness behind Angie's eyes. Besides, she loved the tragic figure of Angie. I'm unsure what her mother had to do to leave her with my mother. I don't remember her

Lizzetta, Deborah, Jacqueline, and Angela at Pacific Ocean Park, Venice, California.

going to a job, but she constantly talked about how dumb Angie was within earshot of my cousin—a comment that my mother resented. We felt ashamed for Angie. So, when she arrived, we'd run to the door and gleefully say, "Angie's here," welcoming her into our modest home, offering her refuge from a mother who, in her concealed rage, never had anything good to say about her beautiful daughter. Though my mother didn't smoke, she believed that those brown ring marks defacing Angie's arms were cigarette burns on the defenseless daughter of this devoted Catholic woman who attended Mass every Saturday like clockwork. The spots were not mosquito bites, as Aunt Ursulina claimed.

On occasions when the shadows of the afternoon passed into the colors of the night, we were all in our PJs, with the lights turned off and our ceramic bunnies on our wall, illuminated thanks to glow-in-the-dark yellow paint when our doorbell rang. It was Aunt Ursulina coming to pick up Angie after school. Sometimes, she wouldn't pick her up on weekends, and we didn't even hear from her until Sunday evening. We liked having Angie over, and even though she was just a year older than me, she seemed more childlike, longing to be loved, as my mother often said.

Eventually, everything unravels in Ursulina's world like a sweater when one critical thread, unnoticed, comes undone. Before you know it, your sweater is half the size it was when you left the house that morning. It was what happened when Uncle Angus grew tired of Ursulina's all-too-often casual encounters with other men. And their relationship was like the sweater; you might as well throw it into the trashcan. But as a child, I didn't know if Uncle was aware of Ursulina's treatment of Angie and the psychological and perhaps physical abuse she suffered. Uncle didn't want to admit that physical violence was a reality in his household. Not wanting to interfere or create a scene, my mother probably told the one person she knew would have no reservations about bringing up the subject, my Aunt Lizzetta, who would confront Uncle Angus and Aunt Ursulina if need be. Aunt Lizzetta was like that if angered. Her black eyes seemed as though they could bore holes right through you—she had no fear. But I don't know—I was a child. Was this one of those hidden secrets in a dark family closet?

Uncle Angus finally divorced Aunt Ursulina, leaving her everything, including the house and the car; he left their daughter Angela to live in that house with his memory alone, with her mother. I asked my mother if he had tried to take her with him. He told her he had, but in those days, the courts felt that children should stay with their mothers in a divorce. Aunt Ursulina also had the Catholic Church and her history with them on her side. The little defense that Uncle may have provided for Angie melted away, and her visits to our home grew fewer and fewer. However, although the vindictive Ursulina owned everything, everything was still not enough.

Uncle Angus remarried when I was away at college, and even though Angie and her father remained close, Aunt Ursulina was not satisfied until she ruined her ex-husband's life. I'd see Angie when I'd come home for visits. Unfortunately, the moonlight of her life dimmed as she fell into heroin use. We tried to pull her back into the land of the living, but she was swimming in waters that were too treacherous for us, an unknown territory we couldn't penetrate. It was a problem for many families who didn't know how to get help. In our neighborhood, rehabilitation and recovery options did not exist, so Angie continued living in a parallel world, disappearing for months and then reappearing unexpectedly.

One December, Uncle Angus and his new wife, Aunt Artie, prepared for their annual Christmas party, a grand affair when Uncle, a sports fisher fan, made a huge pot of seafood gumbo. Then, in all the excitement, Aunt Artie, who was in her early sixties, suffered a sudden asthma attack that woke her up to a pre-dawn gloom that belied the festive holiday décor throughout the house. Her lungs collapsed, and she was dead before the paramedics arrived at their home.

My thoughts turned dark to the pantheon of West African gods unnoticed by slave runners in the memories of enslaved people. They lived in the dark, dank ship hulls with the living, dying, and dead captives, shifting to and fro during the long Middle Passage of the Atlantic as ships threaded their way from the coasts of Africa to the New World. I immediately thought of Aunt Ursulina and a tradition of enslaved people merging their deities with Catholic saints. I wondered if Aunt Ursulina, that child of New Orleans's back streets, was in the house. Did she "put something on Aunt Artie," I shouted, covering my mouth.

The night sky turned purple to black, and the white lights across the Los Angeles basin created a glorious sight as we gathered at Uncle Angus's home. I was happy to see Cousin Angie, but her round, cherubic face with a bright smile was sunken and hollow, and the sadness behind her eyes was now more intense than ever. I stood trying to talk to her, but she was high, sliding into oblivion. I sensed a chill in the air that even she felt.

A rush of coldness draped over me. I stood frozen, frightened, as a black-veiled chiffon figure seemed to float toward me. Darkness surrounded the figure. I wanted to turn away and take flight from this malevolent shape, but my cemented feet sunk into the floor. As everyone else in the room melted away, including Angie, and horrified by the presence of evil, I remained. I could barely breathe—it was Aunt Ursulina's most unwelcome re-entry into my life. She came within inches of my body, her breath touching me, as I watched her long-lashed eyelids lift slowly under her veiled face. I am older and taller now; we make eye contact, and my blood crystallizes at her half-smile and piercing stare. I think she is a powerfully disguised weapon as she gazes into my eyes. She knows that I have discovered her secret and steps backward.

Aunt Phoebe, third from right, at Barksdale Air Force Base, Bossier Parish, Louisiana.

It was my last encounter with her, and poor Angela will not live much longer—she died of an overdose, a possible suicide. Death's fingers finally claimed my uncle's daughter, too.

Uncle Angus moved out of our village, as did Aunt Lena and Uncle Bill, and the youngest daughter, Aunt Phoebe, was the last to come to LA. She married Noel Lebeau and had two daughters while living in Louisiana. In Louisiana, he was in the US Army Reserve based in Bossier Parish in the northwest.

Mom, Aunt Phoebe, and Uncle Booker T were the last three children to leave home. There was little money left by the time they were ready for college. Most of the children left for Los Angeles, but Uncle Booker T's departure was the most challenging for Grandma. After high school, he left Shreveport with his girlfriend and headed for Los Angeles.

"Wilma was my mother's best friend, and she introduced my mother and father in high school [and they married after graduation]. When they came to LA in 1943, seeing the palm trees, she said they had never seen anything so beautiful."

—COUSIN MICHAEL

Uncle Booker wanted to leave Shreveport right after graduating from high school because of a beating he suffered at the hands of a White man at age twelve or fourteen. Some stories, like Grandpa's birth and Uncle Booker T's abrupt departure from Louisiana, remained mysterious for lifetimes. I didn't learn of the trauma he suffered as a young teen until I began writing this book. I always knew him as happy-go-lucky, but I also knew he had a switchblade tucked inside his sock.

"Booker went fishing at the Red River at about twelve or fourteen. He caught some fish and laid them on the bank beside him. A White man came by with his son, who told his father he wanted Booker T's fish. Booker T said, 'No, no, these are my fish.' The White man grabbed Booker T and tied him to a tree. He took off his belt and began whipping him right before his son. The White man took Booker T's fish and went on with his son. It was around 1933. My grandfather witnessed a similar incident when he was about fourteen years old. He and his partner had a job delivering prescriptions. His partner was in the drug store, waiting for a prescription and a little White girl opened the curtain to the back room. She began talking to the Black boy. Whites passing the front of the store saw them talking through the glass window. They got a mob of White men, returned to the store, grabbed the boy, and lynched his grandfather's partner on a light pole in front of the drugstore. White men could do whatever they wanted to Black people. Shreveport was a bad place."

—COUSIN MICHAEL

I read about such tragedies, but my cousin's accounts of these two incidents highlighted the dangers that befell young Black men or boys if they stood up for themselves or were at the wrong place at the wrong time. I wondered how all the Bates children had survived. By the time Booker T reached high school, Grandpa Angus had died, and his influence within the Shreveport community could not protect Booker T.

After Booker T's beating, he became more defiant, but his fearless outer face disguised the hurt that lay in the depths of a troubled man. Family members didn't realize the effects of the beating until many years later. He chose a path of destructive behavior that caused his siblings to watch out for him constantly.

"My father came to LA before joining the service. Aunt Lizzetta and my mother had my father drafted into the army. The draft board sent him to Fort Dicks in New Jersey. My mother and I moved in with Aunt Mabel in Philadelphia to be near him, but my mother divorced him after two years because of his drinking and gambling."

—COUSIN MICHAEL

"You know, Liz, because jobs were scarce, not just for Uncle Booker. So many men from around the country went into the army because they could get a salary."

—MOM

In LA, Uncle Booker T reencountered the same hostilities Whites leveled against Blacks in Louisiana. He took odd jobs on Central Avenue, working at liquor stores. My mother said his friends used to tell him, "Booker, when are you going to stop stealing that liquor from the store?" He'd answer, "You don't have any problem drinking that liquor." He was considered the black sheep of the family. His sisters tried to steer Booker T away from street life but were unsuccessful.

"You always say you 'just trust in the Lord,' but he'd say, 'But see, I can't do that thing. If you don't get it right when you want it, you can go to the bank, and I can't.' He never did have a bank account, and he was just happy-go-lucky."

—AUNT LILLY

"It was Aunt Lizzetta and your mother, Aunt Eloise, who reached out to him in Los Angeles. After my mother divorced him, I did not hear from him. In the late 1940s, he'd come over to take me to Lizzetta's house to spend the night with her. In the 1960s, he changed a little bit and would come over to my grandmother's house at Washington Boulevard and Victoria Avenue in Los Angeles. He would come to Grandma's house and always pull out a bottle of vodka or gin. I don't remember him having a job. He was a street hustler, a very irresponsible person."

—COUSIN MICHAEL

Uncle Booker, tall and slim like Grandma, had exceedingly good looks. Mustachioed with black wavy hair, he looked like he belonged in a Zoot suit as he walked liltingly down city streets. Always a mischief-maker, he thrived on danger from an early age. He teased the bull at the dairy, jumping over the fence into the pen and leaping back before being seared with one of the horns. He barely made it and cut his chin on the rugged wooden railing as he hopped over at the last minute.

Because of his more privileged background in the compound at Lakeside Dairy, Booker T charmed people when sober. He knew how to communicate with the wealthy and those who lived on society's fringes. This skill served him well when managing apartment buildings for some of LA's more affluent Black families. His penchant as a youthful mischief-maker continued well into adulthood. As the youngest of fourteen children, he experienced all the freedoms the youngest child gets—his older sisters adored him and always cared for him, ready to bail him out of financial and other more severe problems. His startlingly good looks helped him to move fluidly throughout social interactions—a ladies' man from a young age, he became someone kept by women throughout his abbreviated life. He sang country-style blues as he moved fluidly through space in a stride that enabled him, with billowing pants around his long, thin legs, tipped with pointed spit-shined shoes, to glide through the streets of Los Angeles. With his older sisters acting as surrogate mothers and his endearing qualities with the ladies, he had time to embark on his other pleasures, such as gambling and drinking, much to the chagrin of his stalwart older sisters. But in his free-wheeling nature, he also had time to create, making collages from large format magazines of the 1950s, like *Life*, *Ebony*, and *Jet* magazines. He'd include all sorts of ephemera, coins he found on the street, medallions from the thrift shop, and inserts of family members into historically significant events.

On the dairy, his siblings remembered him as a playful youth, a favorite son before the beating. That changed him. The following is how I tell Uncle Booker T's migration story because I knew he appreciated observing his surroundings. Sure, he drank, but he liked the wind to hit his face. He noticed the beauty in butterflies and flowers. His creative streak and carefree approach to life were most attractive to me. Although often estranged from his son, Michael, he had a kind and generous nature and was our favorite uncle.

Learning about Uncle Booker T.'s beating alone in the woods while fishing upset me, so I wrote a fictional story about his escape by a train to LA. My husband's uncle also inspired his character, who had to escape Louisiana for Texas after kicking a White man's dog who attacked him. His family and friends helped him to flee through the woods of Louisiana to the Texas border. He never returned to Louisiana. I describe Uncle Booker T.'s observation skills in this micro-story based on how he observed the environment in our small village. I watched and listened to him as he walked in those black-pointed, spit-shined shoes with my mother and sisters from our home to his apartment.

RED CLAY AND BEEF TAMALES

Booker T.'s time to leave came after he stood up to a White man walking by a river tributary with his son. He sat on the bank with his fishing line in the water and two fish he caught next to him. The man's son asked his dad if he could have Uncle Booker T.'s two fish. The man agreed and told Uncle Booker to give him the fish to his son. Uncle Booker said, "No, I caught these fish and don't want to give them away." The White man did not like Uncle Booker refusing his request in front of his son. The man said he was "talking back," but Uncle Booker T stood his ground. After punching Uncle Booker T, the man grabbed him and tied him to a tree with vines hanging. Uncle Booker T fought to get loose, and when he did, he threw rocks from the forest floor at the man and his son, hitting them as they walked away with his fish. The man turned and threatened Uncle Booker T, who grabbed his fishing pole and ran into the thickets of the woods.

When he got home, he told his family what had happened. "Did he know who you are?" his mother asked. "I'm not sure," said Uncle Booker T. At that point, visions of the Black men lynched in Caddo Parish flooded her memory. She knew the man might come back looking to beat, if not lynch, her son. Grandma and his older sisters nursed his wounds, and in the secret of the night, lit by the moon, they ushered him out of Louisiana the back way, behind the empty dairy barn which had closed in 1943 and through the piney woods that smelled of magnolias that shared that wooded space. Grandma had already called two men who worked on the dairy before it closed. They were river people who lived along the Red River. In a small dugout boat, they ferried Uncle Booker T into one of many waterways used since slavery to get out of the South. They knew the ways of the small waterways that ran from northwest Louisiana across the border into East Texas in a small water channel between Shreveport and Waskom, Texas, from Cross Lake. Then, they followed the watery paths near the riverbed until they recognized a clearing in a dense grove of pine trees where the men deposited Booker T. They told him to watch the sky to navigate his way west. Humming cicadas muffled his footsteps as he secretly crossed the border into Waskom the next day to the waiting car of his eldest brother, Bubba (David). The latter had left their family home long ago to start his family dairy. It was much smaller than Lakeside Dairy, but it was enough to sustain his family by raising milk cows and selling milk products to the local families. Most of his dairy business was in Shreveport. Like his father, he trained his sons Hardy and Morris to work on the dairy when they turned thirteen.

Booker T stayed with Bubba just long enough to eat a meal of fried chicken, wash his clothes, and pack a lunch of the remaining chicken for his long journey to Los Angeles. Booker T emerged from Bubba's house in his best clothes and, on his feet, black-pointed, spit-shined shoes. He was ready for his journey. Bubba drove his Buick over three hours to the train station south to Houston so Booker T could board the Southern Pacific Sunset Limited Train from New Orleans bound for LA. He preferred the "Sunset Route" because many Black people had taken that train out of Louisiana bound for LA without any problems. Bubba was like a taxi, dropping off family and friends for their great migration west. Booker T stepped onto the Jim Crow car of the Sunset and headed for Los Angeles as stories of LA filled his head. So many had journeyed west before him, and others would inevitably follow. He was unsure of what LA held for him. When the dairy closed, he was in high school, meaning there was no college money, so he took a job at a hotel. Although he didn't know what to expect in LA, the one thing that Booker T did know was that he had family there that had always taken care of him. He was the baby out of the fourteen children, and as the youngest, you are still the baby, no matter how old you are. He only knew the community around his home, the pine and magnolia trees, the high water behind the barns during the rainy season, the pastures around the dairy farm where the cows roamed before they went into the barn for milking, and the Red River banks where he went fishing with his brother. Everything was new for him.

The train ride was long, and the rocking from side to side reminded him of the old Lakeside Dairy milk wagon, which read Angus Bates Dairy on the side, that old Bert pulled to deliver milk every morning. Bubba told Booker T that Texas was large and wide. The rocking train passed through the dry Great Plains, and the landscape changed slightly from the east to the west. Herds of longhorn steer were a sight to behold. Booker T only knew Holstein and Jersey cows and the black bull he often teased by jumping into his pen until it charged at him. Once, Booker T lost his footing as he climbed the wooden fence, catching his chin on one of its boards before making a final leap over the gate to safety. Remembering his close call to being gored by the bull, Booker T often rubbed the bottom of his chin, feeling the permanent keloid scar as a reminder of his childish act. He was a known prankster, and some of his sisters felt very strongly about his fearlessness.

"Mama should never have named him Booker Taliaferro [after Booker T. Washington]. Booker was a devil."

—AUNT LILLY

When the train reached the desert in the Southwest, there was a familiarity with the place. The clay was red, deposited from sediments in the soil flowing from Oklahoma south to Texas. It reminded Booker T of the days when he sat and fished on the banks of the Red River. The river didn't run by his house but flowed by Cousin Peach's home near Natchitoches, in Redbone country. When his brother Angus lived at home, he'd take young Booker T to visit family on the Red River and fish. Everything was red: the water and the clay. People could tell you had gone fishing by the red stain on the back of your pants from sitting on the red clay bank. Traveling through the dry Southwest's red clay ridges, Booker T wondered if the Red River ran as far as the terraced hills outside his train window. But he was at the Rio Grande, the "big river" that meandered through Texas, New Mexico, and Mexico.

The train crossed the border into California as the sun peeked around the San Bernardino Mountains. "Not much longer," he said to himself. "If anything goes wrong, at least I'll be in California." He didn't know that some places in California were as dangerous for a Black man as the South was. Two things were clear: there were no gold-paved streets, and he was still in the Jim Crow car with all the other Black people headed out West. When his train approached Los Angeles, he saw a long concrete ravine. Was that the Los Angeles River that his brother said he would see just before coming to the train station? It didn't look like a river to Booker T, but what did he know? Maybe Los Angeles had rivers with concrete beds, not red clay like the Red River and the Rio Grande. After all, people talked about the gold streets, and as he peered out of his window, he didn't see any gold. Those who came before him spoke of the cooling waters of the Pacific Ocean along the coast of Los Angeles County. Booker T had seen a map and knew that Los Angeles had reached the ocean's shore. If nothing else, the waters signified the promise of a new life.

Booker T had never seen so many trains and tracks as he did when rolling into Los Angeles's Union Station. Climbing off his train car at his far west destination, a Black porter directed all passengers to the south garden of a tiled station patio adjacent to the waiting room. It was a typical sunny LA day. As he made his way around the front of the station, colorful paper-mâché flowers, piñatas, puppets with sombreros atop their heads, dolls in lace dresses, and the smells of Mexican street foods on Olvera Street greeted him. He bought a handmade tamale from one of the ladies in the brightly decorated stands. Eating the food reminded him of home and Mrs. Beauford, a big, round woman whose mother came from near the Louisiana-Texas border and who made tamales at Christmastime. He was far from home and felt like he was in another country in this land of Pio Pico, the Afro-Mexican governor of Alta California, when it was still part of Mexico. He never considered where tamales came from while eating Mrs. Beauford's, but now he wondered if they came to Louisiana from California.

Booker T stood in front of the station on the rosy Saltillo tiles of the plaza, gazing at magenta bougainvillea trailing along the cream-colored stucco walls up to the red tile rooflines of the buildings. The morning sun soothed his muscles from the rattling train ride that crossed long, flat stretches of the Great Plains and the red scenic terrains in New Mexico and Arizona. He thought about his getaway, navigating the waterways by the light of the moon through the piney woods of northwestern Louisiana that smelled of magnolia flowers, the ride in Bubba's Buick to Houston, and the miles of train tracks behind him.

Booker Taliaferro Bates in Los Angeles.

Relieved, he gazed at the blue sky and the tall, thin palm trees planted along both sides of the street. Watching them wave in the slight breeze, he thought about how this was a different place from home. Then he spotted another Black porter at the curb and said, "Monin. How do I get to Central Avenue?" The porter smiled and welcomed this Southerner, catching Booker T's Louisiana accent. He nodded his head and pointed to a sign that said First Street. Bag in hand, Booker T gestured back with a nod of thanks, and in his best clothes, a bit wrinkled from his long journey and black-pointed, spit-shined shoes, he walked with a confident swagger, heading south.

Remembering Angela, I thought of how welcoming our home was, but all the Bates homes felt like that for family and friends. Most of the two-bedroom California bungalow homes had one restroom that separated the bedrooms with entry doors from each bedroom for easy access. It was a cozy space for my mother, father, and their three girls, who shared the second bedroom. I remember the fun we had with our pillow fights as we hopped back and forth from each other's junior twin beds. Mom furnished our home with hand-me-down furniture from her sisters and whatever she picked up from the thrift shops on Central Avenue. They sold high-quality goods that Black chauffeurs dropped off from their employers in Beverly Hills. Everyone, including Angela, loved to visit.

Mom was a conscientious gardener. Southern Black gardening traditions influenced her garden designs, breaking established rules of symmetrical plantings shown in magazines. Because she and her siblings shared and foraged plants from various sources, especially succulents, they spent little, if anything, on purchasing plants in gardening stores. Instead, they planted collard and mustard greens among their succulents and cacti. Aunt Lizzetta's third husband passed; her male friend frequently drove across the Southern California border to Mexico. He'd return with agave plants and other gifts. Her dry-dirt backyard looked like an orchard of agave with menacing one-inch thorns on large gray-green, water-filled leaves with cream-colored edges. He planted watermelon vines running between the rows. In the plant bed along the side of the house, he planted collard trees always to have enough to make a big pot of greens. Mom and her sisters grew plants in the house too. She was amazed by the different houseplants she could buy in the supermarket, especially the tropical ones. She had them everywhere: in the kitchen, bathroom, living room shelves, the built-in china cabinet, and the dresser tops in both bedrooms, which she consciously tended to each week. When the elderly church ladies came to visit, some commented on the abundance of plants in the house. They disapproved, and they let my mother know.

> "'Eloise, you have so many plants. Aren't you afraid of bugs biting those kids [and] giving them a disease? You shouldn't have so many plants inside with them.'"
>
> —MOM

Mom was much younger than the ladies, so she treated their comments respectfully, but I could tell it bothered her because she'd mention it often, calling them nosey. Besides, she read in used copies of *Ladies' Home Journal* that houseplants improved the oxygen in the house, and she saw her plants as partners fighting the smoke from Pop's cigarettes. So, she quickly forgot about those ladies and didn't invite them into her home again.

Since we didn't own a car, Mom bought a bicycle with a basket on the handlebars and rode it to market. As far as I know, she was the only one in my neighborhood to do so. Of course, people talked, thinking we didn't have the money to buy a car. I admit it; we had little money and a lot of support from my mother's family. Pops caught the bus to work, and my two sisters and I walked to school and everywhere else. Aunt Lizzetta lived a few blocks away. We visited her every Saturday, first stopping by Uncle Booker Ts to grab a handful of candy. He filled up a glass bowl each week in anticipation of our visit before we continued to our aunt's house.

I remember sitting transfixed as Aunt Lizzetta, a natural storyteller, wove stories about the home she and her siblings shared with their parents at Lakeside Dairy. When she finished talking about the cows in the pasture, bringing them in for milking, and taking the milk to market, I felt I knew the place without ever having been there. The milk fermentation process fascinated me. In my Lakeside Dairy moments, I imagined spreading Lakeside Dairy butter on my morning toast, drinking glasses of milk, and my mother eating cottage cheese—which Grandpa also made and sold—to keep her weight down. I smelled and tasted the tart sourness of the yogurt. Products from the dairy, especially yogurt, placed me in my mother's home. Yogurt and the stories about the dairy went hand in hand. Aunt Lizzetta continued with one story after the next, only breaking to rise out of her white leather Queen Ann chair and head to her tiny kitchen for a cup of Thrifty's vanilla ice cream. She returned, nesting in her chair, talking with a bowl of ice cream in one hand with a tablespoon rather than a teaspoon in the other. She told me how they made ice cream at the dairy. But she also told me an easy way to make yogurt: letting it sit in little glass jars on the family's long hearth over the fireplace. Her description of the place was like those I saw in the southwest French country farms I visited as an adult. Also, during visits to her home as an adult, I realized the importance of her staged environment and marveled at the intentional placement of little treasures. I'd sit staring at the colored glass long-neck bottles on her windowsills, which replaced the once colorful stained window glass that the sun used to filter through. They later reminded me of the bottles of remembrance James Weldon Johnson wrote about in his *Autobiography of an Ex-Colored Man.*

Aunt Lizzetta's living room, Los Angeles, California.

"I have only a faint recollection of the place of my birth. At times, I can close my eyes and call up in a dream-like way things that seem to have happened ages ago in some other world. I can see in this half vision a little house—I am quite sure it was not a large one—I can remember that flowers grew in the front yard and that around each bed of flowers was a hedge of varicolored glass bottles stuck in the ground neck down. I remember that once, while playing around in the sand, I became curious to know whether the bottles grew as the flowers did, and I proceeded to dig them up to find out: the investigation brought me a terrific spanking which indelibly fixed the incident in my mind."

—JAMES WELDON JOHNSON[10]

As Aunt Lizzetta's namesake, I realized she was passing her remembrances to me. I was fortunate to be chosen to take her stories into the future. It was a different type of education, one that James Baldwin wrote about in *The Price of the Ticket*, saying, "The education I can receive from an afternoon with Picasso, or from taking one of my nieces or nephews to the movies, is not at all what the state has in mind when it speaks of education."[11]

Aunt Lula on the little boat.

Aunt Lizzetta's collectibles were props for her remembrances and stories about her life at the dairy and her adopted home in Los Angeles. Even as a child, she was set on teaching me lessons, something to carry home with me during these happy moments. Many years later, I realized that she passed them to me for the express purpose of retelling them to anyone who would listen. She didn't want them to be forgotten. So, I didn't forget the stories. I've retold many of them to my children and shared elements of them in my creative writing. One of her favorite stories was *The Little Boat*, about a misadventure her sister Lula had when she and her friend decided to go boating on the lake.

THE LITTLE BOAT

Spring finally came to the dairy, and a sea of late-blooming wildflowers still blanketed parts of the open pasture. While Grandma rested in the shade of the willow tree, Aunt Lula and her friend decided to ride in a boat at the lake's edge beyond the house and the pasture. They walked on a red clay path through the overgrown forest filled with pine trees and towering oaks with outstretched arms dripping with Spanish moss, framing an eerily beautiful view of the open green-blue lake. Louisiana is full of low-country places where you can walk up to the water's edge, a common sight in the southern part of the state; these areas are also typically where many Black people settled, as this was often the only land available to them. Left with the low-water places where the water rose in the rainy season, and the lake, rivers, creeks overflowed, they made do with what they had. These areas that seasonally flooded were called backwater. At some of these home sites, if you didn't encircle your house with lime and keep a large family of cats, aggressive water moccasins and scorpions might venture into the place. It is one reason that Grandma had seven cats—outside cats, who took care of rats, snakes, and all manner of insects.

Growing up at wood's edge, you learned how to take care of yourself; you knew where and where not to walk with bare feet, and you learned about the places where creatures hide, their habits, and their vulnerabilities, as well as yours. You took care to look inside your shoes before slipping your feet into them. You learned about the woods and the waterways, but on this day, Aunt Lula, a tall, pale girl like her mother with long braids folded across the top of her head, "cast her fate to the wind." She had a curious smile that hinted at her exploratory nature and penchant for making risky decisions.

All she knew was that she did it when she wanted to do something. So, even though she didn't know how to swim, she wasn't worried about getting into a small boat on the lake. The two girls did not understand the water currents' character or the tides' ways. But then, she and her friend set out on their journey anyway, through the woodlands toward the little boat on the lake's shore.

Reaching the boat, they collected a few flat pebbles before gingerly climbing in, and with each taking an oar, they set out on their grand adventure. Marveling that they had left the land for water, they watched everything on the shore recede from view—the green woods with pines, oaks, moss, and palmetto trees, the red clay, and all the animals and insects that filled in that habitat. They were gliding through the water above all the animals and water life below. They watched the pelicans as they dove for fish, looked in the water, saw swirling designs, and took turns skipping their pebbles to see who could toss them the farthest. They looked above at the puffy white clouds in the Crayola blue sky with heads bent back. Finally, their eyes settled on the horizon, where

Aunt Lula, 1922.

the sky met the water. They wondered what lay beyond the thin blue line that separated the water from the sky. They were excited explorers, but it seemed farther away as they turned and looked back to the shore. They realized their boat was drifting for the thin blue line, and all they knew was back on the distant green line of the place they had left. Looking again over the water, they could not see the other side. This chilling realization caught hold and turned into panic as they tried to paddle back to shore, but the boat kept wandering farther and farther into the lake. They screamed! Shrills traveled over the water and back to the pasture where the hired hands, John, Dunn, and Henry, were tilling the cowpeas.

George Washington Carver convinced Black farmers to plant cowpeas as a staple for rotation. "The cowpea, rightly handled, is both a bank and mortgage-lifter to the poor man," he wrote in one of the many pamphlets on cooking and agriculture he produced and distributed for free.[12]

Looking up in the direction of the screams, the men remembered seeing the two girls earlier in the day walking up the path—they had exchanged greetings and kept on working. The community children often played in the woods, picking berries and flowers and discovering hideout places and animals and insects that preferred to remain hidden. Black parents cautioned their children about the dangers of the woods and the do-not-cross boundaries. Though everyone felt safe within the confines of the dairy, the limitations of the segregated South remained a constant challenge. Caddo Parish had a history of lawlessness and people disappearing in post-Reconstruction Louisiana. Were the girls abducted? Could a Black person stand up to such an accusation against a White man? A Black person accusing a White man of such a travesty in the twentieth century could mean a severe beating or even prison.

These thoughts ran through the men's minds as they ran up the path to the lake. Then they saw the two young girls in the tiny boat moving out into the water where the unforgiving currents could easily pull them under. These waters had previously claimed other children of the community. The men climbed into a larger boat and headed toward the girls, relieved that they didn't have to endure a situation that could get them beaten, imprisoned, or lynched. These experienced hands in this "sportsman's paradise" were fisher people—crappie, bass, perch, gar, and catfish. Going out on the lake and up and down the Red River was second nature. They had been out on these waters many times with the blue and white herons, pelicans, wild water turkeys, and quail that lived in the shrubs adjacent to the lake. So many were born in river settlements near Natchitoches in Redbone country. The men fished with fishing lines, and when they didn't have that, they caught fish by hand, which they learned from descendants of the Caddo Native peoples who had lived in the area for hundreds of years.[13] The hands fished for supper and caught crawdads for lunch, so saving these girls was a triumph for them and the community. As the larger boat approached the smaller one, the crying girls reached out to the men. They had been so confident as they walked down the path, braving the woodlands, toward the lake. Now, though relieved to be in the safety of the larger fishing boat, all they could think of was the ire of their parents.

Reminded of other tragedies on the water, the men congratulated each other for this rescue—no more deaths to mourn in this community. Not long ago, a young mother started walking along the levee with her three young children. Walking, hiking, and walking into the water, just like the stories of the enslaved Africans walking into the Atlantic Ocean, trying to return to their homes in Africa. Like the Africans, the mother and her three children drowned, were swept away by the water, and were never found. Luckily, the two girls did not meet that fate.

As family members aged, this story and others became a prescient warning to the young. Rather than being a passive listener, I realized the historical significance of the dairy and the associative stories. Thinking back, I feel grateful that Aunt Lizzetta chose me to guide these stories into the future. Amid a separate and unequal life in the South, many joyful everyday occurrences offset the trauma and myth of segregation, where Blacks created their own sense of freedom in those segregated spaces. This story celebrates the carefree days of childhood, the claimed spaces where Black people could be free to interact with the natural environment, reap nature's bounty, explore, and experience the unknown, protected by a community that had their back. Even when you thought you were free, there were those watching you who made sure that your freedom was not interrupted and didn't end in a tragedy.

"[My favorite memories are] playing with my brothers and sisters—ball, hopscotch, jacks, jump rope, somersaults, skates, pickup sticks, and other games. When we would skate, we'd go up all the way to the top of the hill and then roll down fast."
　　—ELOISE

The Little Boat story also had a lasting impression on my mother. Although we did not live near waterways, my mother signed us up for swimming classes at a young age. We continued lessons at several neighborhood pools, often walking to the pool with our neighborhood friends from New Orleans. We all became junior lifeguards. Some of us even saved kids who got in trouble in the water.

While teaching at Tuskegee University, I remember signing my two sons up for swimming lessons at the campus pool. The voice of the coach rings in my head. I watched him as he taught the children how to stroke freestyle. Their narrow arms struggled to pull back the water. "Pull, pull," the coach shouted above the splashing water. Then he yelled, "Swim for your freedom." This coach knew the history of Black people and their relationship to water. It was fraught with challenges, dangers, and sorrow. But it could also mean the joys of splashing tiny feet into rain puddles, running in the rain, and hopping around water released from city fire hydrants when there were no other opportunities to cool off in the urban streets of big cities. It could mean fishing with grandparents or cooling off toes in streams. Or it could mean drowning because many Black children could not swim.

Swim for your freedom conjured up images of aquatic violence, jumping, or being thrown overboard during the dreaded Middle Passage on an enslaver's ship from the West African coast to the Atlantic seaboard, the Caribbean Islands, and South America. However, many enslaved people knew how to swim in rivers and oceans. They connected the sky, rivers, lakes, and seas to represent the universe, creation, and fertility. The water was their friend, a place that got them from here to there, nourished and supported their livelihoods, spirituality, and renewal.

The waters that ran through Southern states were also channels to freedom in the US. For Black people, aquatic spaces were places of resistance to the slavery system, where they found refuge and ran for their freedom. So, how did African Americans lose this critical relationship with water? Many enslaved descendants did not discuss the history of forced bondage in their families. My great-grandmother referred to enslavement as the "dark period." That was all she said.

The boat story reinforced being aware of our surroundings and how elements of nature were constantly changing. Mom taught us to watch for seasonal changes, listen to the birds, and notice the wind on our faces and arms. That knowledge was also inextricably a part of the context of what we grew and ate. Food was essential in my family's migration tales and their longing for environments and communities that bound people together.

Many longtime Black urban dwellers like my family members held onto those memories in their hearts even as they made lives for themselves and their families in major metropolitan centers, which were as challenging and segregated as the places where they were born. In the South, the Jim Crow laws enforced many limitations, governing where Blacks could eat, go to school, shop, or sit on a bus or train. Even so, the movement among Blacks and Whites within those communities was more fluid—they would often walk by and see each other. However, there was very little interaction among the races in many segregated neighborhoods in northern and western centers. Racism was alive and well for those who chose to leave their Southern homes, but good-time memories of those homes sustained them.

I remember the little joys, like coming home from school to find a well-worn brown paper wrapper lying open with pieces of sassafras bark inside, collected from the woods. An aunt, uncle, or cousin had just brought it to our home from their Louisiana trip, or a package arrived by mail. The leaves are dried and crushed to make filé used to thicken gumbo. My mother's family lived in Frierson in DeSoto Parish, where sassafras trees were plentiful. But they were also abundant in Caddo Parish, the site of Lakeside Dairy. But, as with many foraged ingredients, you had to know how to use them. For example, sassafras contains the carcinogenic safrole. Mom didn't know this, but she learned from Grandma to brew tea in small quantities based on traditional brewing knowledge for colds and the flu. She also used it as a topical wash to soothe my itchy eczema and relieve the inflammation. When sassafras was unavailable, we had "kettle tea," one cup of milk, one cup of water, and one teaspoon of sugar. It was like we had gone to the dairy barn to get sweet, warm milk directly from the cows.

Aunt Lizzetta recited family stories, and my mother insisted that we watch the seasons and be aware of the natural changes around us. Hearing them affected how we made decisions and moved through life, like eating sensibly, choosing fresh foods over processed ones, and wearing cotton, silk, or wool instead of synthetic fibers as much as possible. Mom stressed organizing our lives by being mindful of our natural environment while living with the benefits of a modern world. But Aunt Lizzetta was the one who clung onto objects from home as reminders of that place. She was the standard-bearer. As one of the first to leave Lakeside Dairy to work in Los Angeles, she missed her mother's house and didn't want us to forget the pride in owning the only Black Dairy in Shreveport. She also reminded me that she was not always a domestic worker. When the Ye Olde Waffle Shoppe restaurant closed, she turned to a friend who recommended her for a domestic service position, cooking and cleaning wealthy White families' households. She continued in that field until her retirement.

I visited Aunt Lizzetta every week during my childhood and nearly as much when I lived as an adult in LA. One day, as I referred to her as Aunt Lizet, as I had all my life, she said, "Whoever told you that you could call me Lizet? My name is Lizzetta." Astonished, I apologized. She had never objected to me calling her by that shortened name. After many years working in service and now retired, she rejected her White employers calling her Lizet, just as my Aunt Lula rejected them calling her Lulu. They were both proud ladies from a progressive family who

Aunt Lizzetta, Uncle Angus, and Aunt Lilly in Los Angeles.

sacrificed to ensure all the younger children could build sustainable lives for their families. They sent money home to Shreveport for some to attend college. Some needed help to buy automobiles, and others, like my parents, needed help to purchase a house. They sent money to Grandma to fix her roof and sustain her life after the children had gone. And now, my aunts took their names back in the autumn of their lives.

AUNTIE SISTERHOOD

When I was young and innocent
'bout eight or nine I s'pose
I loved to listen to my mom
and aunties speak their prose

Their words to me were [**myoo**-zi-kuhl]
sounds flowing off their tongues
Expressive highs and lows would spew
from deep within their lungs

They'd say things like, "That so-and-so
won't shake a stick at a snake"
Unconcerned to the nth degree
so-and-so would "take the cake!"

"Makin' do," the simple art
of living frugally
If something cost "a little of nothing"
it was close to free

There were times when they would talk
I'll be first to admit
I did not understand a thing
not one tee-ninchy bit

Nonetheless, my ears stayed perked
to take in all they could
To hear those folksy sayings of old
from the auntie sisterhood

Lots of chiming, signifying
"You ain't told no lie!"
They'd be declarin' how they're fairin'
"kickin' but not high"

While I am grown with many years
behind me since those days
I still hold dear the rapture of
their down-home southern ways.

—Deborah LeFalle

THE STARLIGHT COUNTRY SCHOOL AND EDUCATING BLACK CHILDREN

In 1928, in Pasadena, Aunt Lilly visited her classmates from Wiley College in Marshall, Texas. After graduating from Wiley, she returned to Shreveport, where she married Uncle Roy Marcus, and they moved into the Bates home, taking one of the upstairs bedrooms. By that time, three of the older children had moved out. She began teaching at a school in the middle of a canopy of trees, far into the country. A dirt road to and from the school was far different from her college days of fashions, pageants, football games, parties, and the celebrations for the Wiley debate team. But it reminded her of her school growing up in Allendale and the road she and her siblings walked to get there.

> "[I enjoyed] long walks to school in fair weather. If it rained, we took a bus."
>
> —AUNT LILLY

Even though her family's home was at the edge of the Allendale business district, many streets lacked pavement. Sometimes, the bus didn't come when it rained, so she and her siblings had to trudge along the unpaved, muddy road, finally making it home with mud-soaked shoes. My mother often talked about how they'd line up the dirty shoes in a row on the front covered porch. They would leave them until coming out to clean them after dinner the next day. Unfortunately, they would get muddy again if it rained the next day.

Aunt Lilly always wanted to be a teacher, and many teachers' first assignments were remote country "colored" schools. The illiteracy rate was high, and budgets for learning supplies were low due to prohibitions against educating enslaved children before freedom came. In addition, there were no public schools for Black or White children. The Black rural schools suffered from limited essential teaching tools like books, paper, pencils, and other materials that White schools had. The White schools received more financial support and services from the states. During the Civil War, with the infrastructure of many Southern towns destroyed, educational facilities took time to rebound. For Black students, they were not in place. In the early years of the twentieth century, schools remained challenged financially.

Aunt Lilly in Pasadena, California, with friends from Wiley College, ca. 1928, top.

During Reconstruction, Louisiana voters elected Black leader John Willis Menard to the House, but Congress contested the results and refused to seat him. Charles E. Nash was the only Black man elected in Louisiana who went to serve in Congress. Nevertheless, they and some Whites established integrated public schools in New Orleans. But then the Black educators realized that the White teachers teaching in the integrated schools demeaned the Black students, treating them unequally, convincing them they were inferior to the White students. Racism toward Black students and their ability to learn permeated the US educational system for decades nationwide. It was particularly stringent in the Southern states.[14] As she sat in her San Francisco flat, Aunt Lilly often reminisced about that first teaching assignment at the Starlight School.

"My first job was one of the rural schools called Starlight. And we all, the teachers had to have a car that would take us up there. They would pick us up every day. And the man would wait a while and bring us back home. We all paid him to take us up, because it was a school further up from us and he would have to take that group of teachers up to that school. Then he would fool around there all day and they would leave and come back and pick us up. It was two of us, just two of us. The school started by paying us thirty dollars a month, but shortly after that, they raised it to equalize the salaries, and we were getting the same thing the White teacher got, around $350 a month. And all the rural schools didn't run but six months. But I was a governess to a little boy. I would be there in the summertime for Mrs. Guyton. And she had all the best books and everything and would let me read them."

—AUNT LILLY

Even though their pay was low, after saving enough money, Aunt Lilly and Uncle Roy had local Black carpenters, the Doughterys, build a house for them at 506 March Street in Allendale.

In the 1930s, the National Association for the Advancement of Colored People (NAACP) pursued a national campaign to equalize schools and instruction of Black students with that of Whites, saying the "separate but equal" plan, based on the 1896 *Plessy v. Ferguson* Supreme Court decision did not protect their freedoms in the educational system, because Black schools, rural and urban, continued to suffer, especially in the South.[15] Many Black teachers educated in Southern universities migrated outside of the South and enrolled in education programs to earn teaching certificates. Aunt Lilly remembered one of the most difficult decisions of her life.

"[I had to] leave my dear family in Shreveport and go with my husband to California for war work. Being left in Oakland—I had a sister-in-law to help me get adjusted."

—AUNT LILLY

She resided in the San Francisco Bay Area communities of San Mateo, Oakland, and San Francisco before purchasing a home in 1942 in the Fillmore District of what is now known as Lower Pacific Heights. After teaching in a rural Black school in San Francisco, she taught in public schools and, with a love for small children, completed her teaching

Aunt Lilly in San Francisco, California.

career at childrens centers. As a child, every summer, we visited her in San Francisco, especially after Uncle Roy became ill and had to go into care.

Aunt Lilly didn't have any children and survived two husbands. My two sisters and I were her most frequent young visitors. We looked forward to our visits with her because she'd take us shopping on Fillmore Avenue to the Japanese fresh fruit and vegetable vendors and further down on Geary to Japan Town, where she'd purchase us red Tabbies with the tiny metal clasp in the back. These slippers were our annual gift. In addition, Aunt Lilly always bought us paper fans with flowers painted on them, and sometimes a Japanese Geisha doll in Japan Town. Aunt Lilly also had several Buddha figures in her house, and to this day, a carved soapstone lamp of a Chinese wise man holding a cane in one hand and a peach in the other, representing longevity, sits on my table.

She introduced us to Japanese snacks and cookies. When she cooked meals like her standard Cornish hens, she seasoned them with Japanese seasonings, soy sauce, oyster sauce, Mirin, and sesame oil and seeds. Maybe I was curious about my Japanese friends' lunches because of our visits with Aunt Lilly. At lunchtime, many of them brought onigiri rice balls. Often, they wanted what I had for lunch: peanut butter and jelly or cheese sandwiches. But, of course, I liked what they had, so we traded lunches. Like my other childless aunts, Aunt Lilly created opportunities that broadened our world beyond our little village of Louisiana and Texan cultures in Los Angeles.

So, even though we were limited to where we could move in Los Angeles, we learned about other cultures through objects like Aunt Lizzetta's French collection embossed with fleur-de-lis. As a collector of French antiques, I think she liked its lily shape. I doubt that he knew that the design's history related to enslavement in the French colonial period in Louisiana. In 1724, Louisiana adopted Black Codes like those in other French colonies to discourage runaway enslaved Africans. The fleur-de-lis was a property brand initiated by Napoleon Bonaparte, who branded the shoulders of those he enslaved, signifying their status as runaways. Part of their punishment included cropping their ears. He sold the Louisiana French colony to the United States. But Aunt Lizzetta probably saw early images of the fleur-de-lis on the cardboard covers of their school pictures.[16]

We looked forward to the drive to the Hollywood Methodist Church's International Days at that massive Church—volunteers dressed in ethnic clothing to represent many countries in Europe and South America. Unfortunately, there may have been only one representative from the continent of Africa. In the late 1950s, Black or even African representation was not widespread. But aside from the costumes, they sold cookies, other sweets, and dolls dressed in ethnic clothing from many cultures. They also sang songs in different languages. It was always fun and another opportunity to expand our horizons despite the limitations imposed on Black people. But you must dream beyond the obstacles.

Although I grew up hearing the rumble of trains across the street from my LA home, I had never ridden one like my parents. Aunt Lizzetta took my cousin Michael back to Shreveport, probably since his father, my Uncle Booker T, was a wayward fellow. Michael was a city boy like I was a city girl.

"On the train, Aunt Lizzetta took me to Shreveport in 1946, but when we got to the South, we had to change seats [they had to move to the Jim Crow car]. The house still had two stories. You could look out the kitchen door and see the dairy barn and cows grazing. I was afraid of chickens. So, they'd put chickens under the house so I could go outside."

—COUSIN MICHAEL

I always thought of Daddy's stories of his train rides and all my relatives who took trains from Louisiana. I only knew about these land-scapes through them because I lived in the city. Daddy's stories opened spaces I didn't know existed, but I guessed as a child the vast landscapes were probably something he didn't know existed before becoming a Red Cap. He lost his parents as a child and was raised by his older sister until he became a young man and struck out on his own to make discoveries in other places and landscapes. He went west because part of his family also migrated to LA. He stayed with his father's sister before marrying Mom. The Pacific Ocean was the end of the trail. When you leave your family home and everything and everyone you know, you can redefine yourself and be whoever you want to be. He did just that and changed the spelling of his last name from Leffall to LeFalle. His family in Texas always wondered why.

DADDY'S MISHAP ON THE RAILS WITH CHICKEN

My fascination with riding the train, fed by my mother's accounts of riding the train from her home in Shreveport to Los Angeles during the Great Migration West, fueled my imagination. Daddy also told us stories about "running the road" as a Red Cap for Southern Pacific Railway. He told one story, over and over, about train stops at different points in the South where Black folks couldn't get any service from food vendors. Most brought their food with them, often fried chicken. Customers raised windows to buy food from the Black vendors at train stops for those who didn't have or ran out of food. This practice began after Civil War with enterprising Black women known as "Waiter Carriers." They served train passengers plates of food near the train tracks across from the Gordonsville, Virginia, train station platform.[17]

Daddy said Black vendors appeared at train stops selling portable fried chicken packages on his route from Texas to LA. But in some places, trains couldn't stop. They slowed down. As the trains pulled up, porters and Black passengers reached out of their Jim Crow passenger cars, first throwing money to the vendor for their meal. Sometimes, the stop was very brief, and all the vendors could do was hang a bag of fried chicken on a hook that was reachable by Red Caps, who would throw them money for the meal.

One time, Daddy was hungry and ready to eat some crispy Southern fried chicken. He got all his change from the tips he made from carting passengers' luggage onto and off the trains. He knew the train stop in Texas, where a vendor would hang a bag of fresh fried chicken on the hook just before the arrival of the train. Of course, it wasn't a train stop, but the train slowed down so the tracks could change direction and then continue to Los Angeles. Daddy said the Black people were excited about their journey and arrival in LA. There, they would reconnect with family members who had gone there before them and who wrote letters of great stories and opportunities they enjoyed once leaving the South. Riding the road back and forth from Los Angeles to Texas, he knew that everything wasn't as rosy as some of the stories professed, but it was far better than the South. The educational and employment opportunities they sought were not available in the hometowns where they came from. Anyway, back to the fried chicken.

Daddy could almost taste the fried chicken as the train pulled up to where the conductor changed the tracks. He could see the greasy paper bag in the distance and prepared himself to stretch his arm for the long reach to the bag. He had to position himself just right to grasp the bag without tearing it and losing his chicken. As the train approached slowly, he took his money out of his pocket and tossed it to the chicken vendor below at the right moment. Then he grabbed the chicken off the hook. He waved a hand, thanking the man for the chicken, and returned to a train car to enjoy his meal. Sitting down, readying himself for a delicious eating experience of fried chicken, he thought of his family home in Elysian Fields outside of Marshall, Texas, and the chickens they cooked.

Then, he bit into the chicken and crunch! He hit something hard, almost breaking his tooth. He thought he had bitten too hard and hit a chicken bone, so he took another bite. Crunch again! He hit another bone. He peeled back the crispy batter and could not find any meat. He tried another piece, and the same thing happened: crunching, only biting on bones. Then he began to pull all the crispy batters from all his chicken. There was no meat. The so-called vendor fooled him. Though deliciously tasty, he only had crispy chicken skin and no chicken. He sat there in disgust but was still hungry, so he ate the crispy chicken skin, wiped his hands and mouth, and returned to work.

Turnip Greens with Bottoms. Illustration by author.

TURNIP GREENS WITH BOTTOMS

Many people do not like turnip greens, but we ate them with glee. When I got older, I often heard people coaxing their children to eat vegetables, especially green ones. That was not the case with us. As children in

LA, we ate collard, mustard, and turnip greens. Was it because we were introduced to their taste by the pot "likker" (the residual liquid left after cooking greens) scooped from the pot into our cups to drink? Don't forget the hot water cornbread, an excellent accompaniment for the pot "likker."

Hands-on time: 15 minutes
Total time: 1 hour
Serves: 6

Ingredients:
   1 ½ cups yellow onions, diced
   3 bunches of turnip greens, thoroughly washed, with stems
      stripped
   3 cups small to medium-sized turnip bottoms or bulbs, diced to
      medium size (approximately ½-inch pieces)
   2 cloves garlic, chopped
   1 quart chicken stock
   ¼ cup canola oil or other oil
   1 cup cubed salt pork (cut rind and remove and rinse off the salt)
      or bacon
   2 bay leaves
   2 tsp. kosher salt
   1 tsp. of black pepper
   ½ tsp. crushed red pepper
   2 Tbsp. apple cider vinegar

Preparation:
   In a large pot, render the salt pork or bacon; add onion and garlic and cook until soft. Add greens, chicken stock, and bay leaf; cook on high until boiling. Turn down the heat to low and simmer, covered, for approximately 45 minutes or until greens are tender. Add water if needed. Remove about one cup of pot "likker" and place in a medium-sized pan with enough water to cover and cook bottoms. Cook on medium heat until tender, roughly 15 minutes. Add the bottoms to greens and season to taste with salt, black pepper, red pepper, and apple cider vinegar.

Hot Water Cornbread.

HOT WATER CORNBREAD

This quick cornbread recipe goes well with any pot of greens, cabbage, beans, or even tomato-based stews. It is the first cornbread dish I learned to make and one of the most satisfying that reminds me of Mexican fried masa or Indigenous fried, corn-based bread. Unlike traditional cornbread, there are no eggs, milk, baking powder, or sugar. Instead, it is just cornmeal, water, baking soda, and salt and pepper if you wish. Sometimes, I make mine savory with cayenne pepper or paprika. I don't usually measure my ingredients, but here is a basic rule of thumb for about five three-inch-long pieces of bread.

Hands-on time: 10 minutes
Total time: 10 minutes
Serves: 6–8

Ingredients:
    1 cup cornmeal
    ½ tsp. salt
    ½ tsp. pepper, optional
    ½ tsp. baking soda
    ½ cup water
    ½ cup of canola oil

Preparation:

Mix dry ingredients in a large bowl. Add water until the dry mixture is moist enough to roll into a ball and pat it into an oval shape about 5/8 inches thick. The mixture should stick together and not fall apart, but it should not be wet or mushy. Pour the canola oil into a medium to large cast-iron skillet over medium-high heat. Place two to three paper towels on a plate to place the fried bread after removing them from the hot oil. Place all patties on a plate while the oil is heating. When the oil is hot, gently lower each patty into the hot oil. This way, you will ensure crispy edges. You may have to fry your bread in batches. The oil should bubble around each patty.

Using a spatula, check your pieces of bread after about 4 minutes to ensure they are frying to a golden brown before gently turning them over. The bread should have a lightly browned crust. Test the center of each patty with a fork, butter knife, or long toothpick. The inside should be softer than the outside crust but not mushy. Remove each one to the paper towels using a spatula to drain the excess oil. Top each hot patty with a smear of butter and sprinkle lightly with salt. Serve immediately, and whatever you are serving them with, ensure you include a nice helping of pot "likker."

AUNT LILLY'S CORNISH HENS

Writing this narrative, I realized that the baked Cornish hens Aunt Lilly served on every visit were northwestern Louisiana favorites. I knew they were always on the menu whenever we visited her in San Francisco. My sisters and I teased each other, whispering if she would serve us anything other than those little birds. But no, supper was always baked Cornish hens, a side vegetable, and Rice-a-Roni, advertised as "the San Francisco treat." But I think she served so many meals of Cornish hens because perhaps they reminded her of the roast duck meals she ate for breakfast and supper in Louisiana. They were plentiful because her father was a duck hunter.

Hands-on time: 10 minutes
Total time: 1 hour, 15 minutes
Serves: 4

Ingredients:
3 to 4 Cornish hens
¼ tsp. cayenne pepper
¼ tsp. black pepper
¼ tsp. garlic powder
½ tsp. soy sauce
½ tsp. sesame oil
¼ tsp. salt or Creole seasoning

Preparation:
Preheat oven to 375°F. Wash and pat dry hens with paper towels. Place the hens in the pan and sprinkle salt and pepper in the cavities and on the outside of the hens; coat the hens with liquid seasonings, then add the dry ones. Cover the pan with foil. Bake for 50 minutes. Remove the foil and return it to the oven until golden, about 15 minutes longer. You can also cook the covered hens in an oven-safe casserole pot. Prepare a box of Rice-a-Roni and serve with the hens for a San Francisco treat. You can also put the partially cooked Rice-a-Roni around the hens for the last 15 minutes of cooking.

Chapter Two

A RESIDENCY IN A
FRENCH VILLAGE

AS FAMILY MEMBERS AGED, I KNEW I'D HAVE TO MAKE TIME TO PUT
pen to paper and write down all their memories and stories about the
dairy. My time was running out before they left this world. I had to act
now. After completing a complex curatorial project, the dairy was on
my mind. I longed for a place where my creative mind could wander
and meander through those stories. I thought of why my mother fed
us yogurt and kefirs and realized it was a way of returning momentarily to what she knew from her childhood at the dairy. Because of
the storytelling tradition in my family, I wanted to assume the role of
storyteller for my family. I wanted to strengthen my creative writing
skills, so in 2006, I applied for an artist residency in a small village in
the Aude region of southern France, in Sainte Colombe sur l'Hers, to
develop a website telling the stories of contemporary artists. Little did
I know that this tiny French village with serene hills and a gently slop-
ing landscape with curvy two-way roads would become the catalyst
to embark on my journey of discovery and intimate relationship with
Lakeside Dairy. I realized I had created a career of telling everyone else's
stories, so why not tell my own? It was a Lakeside Dairy moment in a
small farming village in southwest France. After many days of walking
in the countryside, I returned to my studio, exhaled, and began to write.

Once arriving in Sainte Colombe, I relaxed in my studio, where I'd
write for the next month. A sensation welled up in my chest. I felt that
I had been in this place before—indeed spiritually because I had not
been in France physically for over ten years and had never traveled
outside of Paris. My grandparents' dairy was in my thoughts. Is that

why I am in this place? The yellow, orange, and red trees blanketed the countryside in the fall, with small farms tucked among the rolling hills. In my childhood, it was the yogurt-eating season. For some reason, the environment in the village reminded me of the stories family members told me as a child. The small community also reminded me of the neighborhood of my youth, where families shared memories and values of their Southern upbringing and walked to their homes to greet each other. So, I began writing *Seasons at Lakeside Dairy*. Aside from memoir and storytelling, my book is also a migration tale, as I explore the core sense of longing for environments and communities that bound people together. Many new and long-time urban dwellers hold memories of their Southern homes in their hearts, even as they made lives for themselves and their families in major metropolitan centers. I consider how my family conjured home through gardens, food, and objects.

I thought about Lakeside Dairy again as I rode my bike through the countryside of Sainte Colombe. Seeing the cows, sheep, and goats reminded me of rural life in general and my grandparents' dairy. Southern France ushered in another chapter of my life as I followed the yogurt that led me to this story. Most yogurts and cream come in little glass jars in France, and although smaller and shaped differently, they reminded me of the small glass milk bottles that lined Aunt Lizzetta's mantle. Small milk bottles, given to me by my aunts and mother, now stand on my shelves as testaments to Lakeside Dairy.

US Blacks and their relationship with farming and gardening and the stories learned from their families quickly entered my consciousness. The topic of sustainable farming practices in France led me to talk to farmers and jot down questions for my mother, as my experiences carried me further into food and a network of farmers sustaining the needs of their village. Farmers spoke of supporting the needs of their villages, but with fewer farmers than before and the rise of the supermarket, it was easier to get many goods. Most of the fresh food at Lakeside Dairy came from my grandparents' farming and community members, but they bought staples like flour, sugar, and salt from the local markets.

Driving through this scenic valley in southwestern France, I pondered why I was here and realized I was to find Lakeside Dairy in this countryside. Recalling one aunt after the other as they retold memories, mimicking them in my mind, saying their words silently, not moving my lips to offend the storytellers, but wondering, why are they telling me this again? Finally, their memories spilled onto my paper at my studio's writing table. I was supposed to memorize the stories to pass them on. Documents are often lost, especially as people migrate from one place to another, so we commit essential things to memory.

As a child born on Christmas day, when the nuns sang carols as they walked down the halls of Queen of Angels Hospital, I have always felt I am the one who is supposed to remember. This realization was almost too much to bear—I only had a month to organize my writing outline and to jot my ideas down. Coming to this point had been a journey, and my text was in a state of becoming—it wouldn't happen quickly. So, I wrote several shorter stories and called them my Lakeside Dairy moments. *A Short Walk Through the Corn Fields* is one of my Lakeside Dairy moments when I lived in Sainte Colombe sur l'Hers.

A SHORTCUT THROUGH THE CORN FIELDS

The living quarters and studios were separate from each other. I chose the smaller apartment in the compound, Les Buis, because my media project didn't need many workspaces, and I didn't have much money. When I opened the single French door and saw the fireplace hearth, I thought of Grandma's clabber that sat in a container on her mantel, away from drafts, until it was acidic. I thought of the teacakes made with real butter churned from the dairy cows. Lakeside Dairy was on my mind.

Some days, I walked out of my compound and headed straight up the dirt road; by this time in the fall, it was filled with yellow leaves that had floated to the ground, covering the path from the chestnut tree limbs above. Waving my bonjour to the jolly man and his wife renovating their stone home, I cut through cornfields about seven city blocks to La Forge, the location of the center's office and additional residential housing and studios. Before walking home, I'd meet with Rosa, a poet from Spain, and stop and pick a few Comice pears from one of the trees at the center's small orchard. And then, farther down the road, a quince tree stood near the sculpture studio. Although I loved quince paste, I had never made any; my husband's aunts were also from northern Louisiana, and like my mother's family, they made quince jam. So, I quickly picked some quinces, threw them in my backpack, and headed home to email my husband, asking him if he remembered the recipe. He did. The following day, I took off writing and began making the jam.

I ensured I had all the necessary ingredients and tools; I remembered French chefs' refrain of "mise en place," putting all my cooking tools and ingredients in place before beginning the cooking process. Luckily, I checked that I had a blender in my closet-sized kitchen before picking the fruit. I washed, deseeded the quinces, and cut them into cubes. After puréeing the cubes in the blender, I boiled, simmered, and canned them in small glass jars I had purchased on market day. To my delight, the jam tasted like the expensive quince pastes I bought in one of those overpriced gourmet markets. The texture was different, but the taste was the same. That afternoon, I walked down the road to the little village store to buy a fresh baguette. I chatted with the older ladies in their aprons, looking like they had just left their kitchens to buy a baguette for that night's dinner. I told them about my success with the quince jam in broken French. The next day, I spread my jam on baguette pieces and shared it with the ladies at the corner store. They seemed impressed, and some offered suggestions for making spicy versions. I felt like I was a part of the village, standing in front of the market, chatting about my culinary feat. I remember having quince jam as a child, probably at Aunt Lizzetta's house. She was infamous for serving us jam on toast; most jams came as gifts from Shreveport. The fruit trees that grew in her family's orchard at their dairy home developed her taste for fruit jams and preserves.

Originally from Turkey, quinces were regularly included in still-life paintings and drawings from the ancient times of Pompeii into the twentieth century. Early European settlers probably brought its seeds to the US like many other fruits and vegetables.[1]

My grandmother had an original "long yard" chromolithograph print, *A Morning Treat-Fruit*, by J. Giovanni Califano, above her fireplace

J. Giovanni Califano, *A Morning Treat-Fruit*, 1907.

hearth. I imagine my aunts and uncles looking at that print and comparing the fruits to what grew in their orchard. So, *A Short Walk Through the Corn Fields* was the story that I told my children because I want them to pursue a similar international experience. But, by extension, it was a dairy story, a Lakeside Dairy moment.

Chunky Quince Spread. Illustration by author.

CHUNKY QUINCE SPREAD

Quince jam is an acquired taste that I first experienced through my husband's family. In Ouachita Parish, Louisiana, his aunts picked and prepared quince jam. It is one of those recipes that benefit from working clean. After several failures when canning fruits in glass jars, I knew I needed to "work clean," as chef Anthony Bourdain reminded his kitchen staff. Be sure to organize ingredients and tools and wipe them up after each step. Note: I don't use pectin, but add water according to the package instructions if used.

Hands-on time: 45 minutes
Total time: 1 hour, 30 minutes
Yield: 8 jars

Ingredients:
  5 fresh large quinces (about 6 cups), cored, peeled, and chopped
    into 1-inch chunks
  5 cups sugar (I prefer tart, chunky fruit spreads rather than overly
    sweet ones. Add more sugar to your taste.)
  4 cups water
  1 Tbsp. lemon zest
  ¼ cup lemon juice

Preparation:
  Sterilize 8 half-pin-sized glass canning jars in boiling water. Place
  a flat dish in the freezer to test the readiness of the quince mixture.
  Place the quince chunks in a large pot, pour cold water over them,
  and bring them to a boil. Reduce the heat to low and simmer covered
  for 15 minutes; strain off the juice (about 4 cups). Add lemon zest and
  lemon juice to the fruit. Reduce the heat and simmer the quinces
  and citrus until soft. It will take about 10 to 15 minutes. Strain the
  juice from the quinces. Discard the quince pulp and save the juice if
  you want something like paste. If you want a chunky quince spread,
  keep the pulp and mash with a potato masher.
  For both processes, stir in the sugar and boil again. Lower the
  heat to medium-high and cook the quince liquid for about an hour,
  stirring occasionally. Taste for desired sweetness. At this point, add
  more sugar or lemon to taste. Turn off the heat when the mixture
  thickens. Take the plate from the freezer and drop a teaspoon of the
  mixture onto the dish. If the jam runs in the dish, it's not ready, so
  continue cooking. Spoon the hot spread mixture into the sterilized
  canning jars and seal it. Label it and store it in a cool, dry place.
  Refrigerate after opening.

Chapter Three

SEASONS AT LAKESIDE DAIRY

"Dad worked seven days a week and 365 a year. Rain, shine, sleet, or snow. There's no letting up in the dairy business. No time for socializing. He sold mostly to Whites because the Blacks didn't have money for the dairy. All the customers were White. We had Grade A milk certified by the City of Shreveport. We milked cows daily at 4:30 a.m. and bottled the milk in tall glass bottles and delivered milk around the entire city of Shreveport. We made a cream cheese and sour cream, by letting the milk sour and separating the sour cream and clabber. We pour the sour cream in a small glass half-pint bottle and pour the clabber into a mold (tin with holes), allowing the liquid clabber to drip through the tin cans with holes, creating a round cream cheesecake about three and a half inches round and about one inch thick. Both were sweet due to the sweet milk, milked from the cows for many years. Angus Bates, [with a limited formal education, used other skills to succeed in] owning and operating of the Lakeside Milk Dairy for around thirty-five years until his death, December 7, 1935."

—UNCLE ANGUS

Tall and commanding, with a straight nose, silken curly hair, suntanned caramel-colored skin, and gray eyes, Angus "Pat" Bates built the two-story, five-bedroom house on a corner of Talbot Street and encircled it with fruit and nut trees in the Black neighborhood of Allendale, in Caddo Parish in Shreveport. His friends and close family members called him Pat, older cousins called him Cousin Pat, but we knew him as Grandpa.

Grandpa Angus Bates and the concrete silo in the back with his initials, AB.

"We lived in a big two-story house. There were four [or five, because Grandpa added rooms as the family grew] bedrooms and only one bathroom. There was a big hall that went through the length of the house. There were two back porches with large backyards and a big front yard with a brick sidewalk from the front porch to the front gate. In the backyard, there were chicken coops and a beautiful covered well. Our home was happy."

—AUNT LILLY

One of Shreveport's earliest subdivisions was small family lots when Grandpa built his dairy. The area constantly flooded because flood-plains ran through many neighborhoods, with water rising as high as the porches and into some houses. As with most places undesirable to Whites, Grandpa had to navigate those undesirables and make them desirable for his diary business and family home. He built his house on

Aunt Lilly (front) and Aunt Janice (Beaut).

a hill to stave off as much flooding water as possible. But his elevated house was also where he could sit on his porch and marvel at the space he created for his animals and family at day's end.

"My loving parents did everything to make our childhood days happy. There were horses to ride, and there was always plenty of space for our friends. We had large barns and lots of pastureland. My two older brothers helped with the dairy, and we always hired help."

—AUNT LILLY

The Bates family had more than other families in the area. The local folks wondered about Grandpa. "Pat Bates," the people would say, doesn't look like any Bates from around here. There were always whispers when the baby suddenly became a part of the family. After emancipation,

Grandpa's only known father, John Bates, came to sharecrop in Louisiana from a South Carolina plantation. Speculation is that before the Civil War, he was a free man, but then, like so many freemen, he was captured and enslaved during the war. When freedom came, John left South Carolina and, like many Blacks and Whites from Southern states in the east, settled in the uplands of Louisiana to farm the land. He married, but they were childless, and when an infant became available in their community, they took the baby boy, raised him as their own, and named him Angus Bates.

"Father was born in a little four-room house on the corner. He belonged to a little Baptist Church—Pleasant Grove Baptist Church [which he helped build]."

—AUNT LILLY

Raising someone else's child was common, especially if the father was unknown. Although they didn't say it wasn't their child, people knew. They had seen this before. Great-grandma's sister was brown-skinned, and John Bates was mulatto. People gossiped. Grandpa was about five shades lighter in the winter, and three in the summer, and his hair of dark silken curls didn't sit right with some folks. People didn't know Grandpa's father but were convinced it wasn't Mr. Bates. They assumed that he was another man's child. Grandpa didn't discuss it, and folks knew not to ask him.

Louisiana and Texas were similar destinations for enslavers bringing their enslaved persons west to head off capture by the Union Army. This migration, forced or voluntary, highlights the enslaved population's continuous movement across the US in search of freedom and sustainable lives. Consequently, after freedom came during Reconstruction, Blacks from older Southern states like Virginia, the Carolinas, and Georgia moved west to Southern states that needed more laborers and had more competitive wages than those in the old South. New Southern states, like Mississippi, Louisiana, Texas, and Arkansas, received these laborers and paid them more to cultivate cotton.

Investigating family history reveals new information, especially with Black people whose family trajectory is anything but straight. Enslavement made it challenging to identify one's ancestors further than one or two generations back. However, as I delved deeper into both sides

State of Louisiana Tax Receipt, 1907.

of my family, I realized that similarities put the families on the same trajectory. Both sides were brought west by plantation owners, one from South Carolina and the other from Georgia, as the Union Army fought the Confederate Army, pushing plantation owners from their land and freeing the enslaved people in their path. Realizing the potential of losing their valuable enslaved property, the owners sent enslaved persons to live with family members in west Louisiana, Arkansas, and Texas.

My mother's matriarch and my father's grandfather experienced this westward movement trail with their owners, who hoped they could maintain their slave-owning way of life by keeping their human property enslaved elsewhere. Enslavers brought my mother's family to northwest Louisiana, Frierson in DeSoto Parish, and my father's family to Elysian Fields near Marshall in northeast Texas. According to Uncle Angus, Grandpa's namesake, his father moved to Shreveport in 1897 and married Grandma Carrie D. around 1901 after his first wife, Rose, died and left him with two small children, Lena and Leonard. He and Grandma Carrie D. had twelve children and welcomed the two children from his previous marriage. While his children from his first marriage lived with Rose's family most of the time, they were welcomed into his new home with Carrie D. and often visited as the two sets of children merged.

Grandpa drove a delivery wagon as a young man and then was a milker and delivered milk for Miller Dairy. But as his chores at the dairy increased, he learned the trade of dairy farmers by watching and doing. Grandpa prepared the cows for milking, fed them, cleaned stalls, fixed the fences in the pasture, and everything else needed to keep that dairy running. Nobody trained him to be a dairy worker; he silently listened, learned from his boss, and saved his money. Then, to everyone's surprise, Grandpa Angus opened his dairy in 1907 with one cow and one bull. He paid his first business tax on the dairy in 1908.

When Grandpa became an entrepreneur with his Lakeside Dairy, tongues were wagging again, especially in Allendale; they wondered how the younger Bates earned enough money from driving that old milk wagon to open his own business. Folks finally figured out he was doing more than driving that horse-drawn milk wagon all over town. Grandpa Angus also worked at the dairy. And in doing so, he learned about the dairy business.

"Through the years, his dairy grew to forty cows and three bulls."
—UNCLE ANGUS

THE FIRE OF 1925

More than a farm, Lakeside Dairy was a haven, a sanctuary for a family of twelve and sometimes fourteen. The dairy ran from Cross Lake to Allendale-Lakeside, where Black folks settled in Shreveport, Louisiana. When my mother was born in 1924, the second to the last of Carrie D. Bates's twelve children, the following year, on September 4, 1925, just shy of her first birthday in November, a nighttime fire ignited in Allendale, destroying about two hundred homes. Why did so many homes burn to the ground? The culprit was a broken water main that could not water the Allendale community. The fire lit up the night sky as the children watched its yellow and orange glow, wondering if it would come to them. As they watched, their parents hatched a plan. They would gather a few belongings and head for the lake if it came too close. Grandpa instructed John, Dunn, and Henry, the hired hands who lived in the little barn near the large barn that housed the cows, to release them, their horses, and chickens into the fields away from the house. They whistled for their dog, Red, to follow them to the lake's edge. Red couldn't fit in the boats, but at least he had a chance to swim at the water's edge. The family and men got into the two small boats, paddled into the lake, and remained there, hoping the fire would not reach the house and barns. As dawn broke and much of the haze from the fire's smoke rose, they could see their barns in the distance and, farther away, their family home. They were still standing. They paddled back to the grassy bank and climbed out with their belongings. Red came running to them, splashing in the water. He had remained at the edge, just as they suspected he would. The family and hands could hear their cows mooing in the distant pasture, realizing that some, if not all, were still alive. The smoke was still heavy, so they waited in the boats until the wind-driven fire changed direction and blew away from their home. As the smoke thinned, they trudged back to their home.

Grandpa noticed one of his fire-singed fences in front of the house, but the old fig tree, with its large, green, water-filled leaves, took the brunt of the fire, disabling it from reaching the home. Other people closer to town were not so fortunate. The Bates family lived near its end as it edged to rural pastures. The business district and homes close to downtown Shreveport caught fire; more than a thousand people were left homeless. At that time, there were not many Black families living in Allendale. Most of the residents were immigrants from Italy, mainly Sicily. Also, immigrants from Greece and Lebanon lost their homes.[1] In this case, segregation saved this Black family.

Even more ominous than fire, the rain was a major cause of flooding in the lands around the dairy. Some years during the rainy season, the bayous and Cross Lake overflowed and covered all the pasturelands, almost reaching the giant fig tree behind the dairy barn and the path to the house, which turned into slippery mud when it rained. I often thought about the Bates family siblings, walking back and forth from the big two-story home to the dairy barn behind the house as I tried to rediscover their world. I thought about their relationship to the land and the subtropical environment, the sweetness of a country morning, what they sacrificed when they migrated from the Southern United States to urban centers in the Northeast and the West, and what they reconstructed to make their new homes. Conceptually, LA to LA (Louisiana to Los Angeles) could have been a better leap. The two places shared geographical, environmental, and cultural commonalities. They both had subtropical climates. Louisiana has moist tropical air in spring and summer and cold air in the winter. At the same time, LA's weather is classified as a Mediterranean climate, with subtropical dryer summers and mild rainfall during the winter months.

The Spanish empire claimed both Southern California and south-western Louisiana. Los Adaes Mission and a fort (presidio) served as the capital of the Province of Texas for forty-one years. It became a part of western Louisiana where the Spanish, French, Blacks, and Caddo Indigenous peoples coexisted together, actively trading goods to sustain their lives.[2] Both LA and southwest Louisiana have a folk tradition from Mexican migrants. Making tamales especially resonates with me, as food is the vehicle my family uses to connect culturally to both places.

In the late nineteenth and early twentieth centuries, Black people in Louisiana were mainly tenant or sharecropper laborers tied to cotton production in the North and sugarcane in the South. Their dwellings were temporary structures to house the non-landowning families as they moved from one location to another. Significantly, Black people in rural Shreveport near Lakeside Dairy sharecropped land. But Grandpa owned his home and pastureland to graze his cows. He held so much land that he rented out space to other people for their farm animals. So, as Black people moved out of the South for better opportunities, his family had everything they needed on the dairy. Most people who owned land had large families to maintain it. And as his children grew, he employed them on the farm. He paid them a small stipend to help them to learn that they should receive payment for their labor. By consulting census figures for my family beginning in 1910, I saw how the family dairy developed and who was employed and lived on the dairy.

According to Uncle Angus, people were surprised that Grandpa could buy a hilly parcel of land on Talbot Street between Hartman and Holzman Streets. He had enough area for pastureland to graze his dairy cows and other cattle. Grandpa branded all his livestock with his initials, AB, using a "branding iron," a long iron rod with his initials. He heated it in the fire until red hot and pressed it against his cow's hide, marking livestock to identify his ownership. The cows only took up part of the property. Plenty of land was left to plant vegetable crops like turnip and collard greens, cabbage, crook neck squash, lima beans, black-eyed peas, red beans, corn, and fruit and nut trees. Farming and dairy were the family's bread and butter. Being a Black farmer in the Southern US meant one had to be cautious in purchasing substandard seeds,

Aunt Lula with a colt on the dairy.

affecting crop yield and value. It was one of many deliberate ways to keep them from competing with White farmers. Their trusted sources for seeds were often those tested by historically Black colleges, George Washington Carver's Jessup Wagon, and other proven and laboratory-tested sources.

When I talk to people about the dairy farm, they first mention lactose intolerance among Black people. I admit I am suffering from this fate, but it was not always the case, and this disorder did not affect my mother and her siblings growing up on Lakeside Dairy, so what happened? Of course, back then, family farming methods required patience and understanding of the whole picture of the landscape. Today, it's called permaculture. Cows promoted biodiversity by eating the grass in the pasture, making way for ground nesting and larger birds.

The most successful method of sustaining Grandpa's dairy farm was diversifying his farming operation. Carver championed these methods as he traveled to rural communities in Alabama and neighboring Southern states, attending meetings and talking to farmers about their crops and livestock. He told farmers to rotate their crops to allow the soil to breathe and to plant beans and peanuts to replace minerals depleted from the ground because of single-crop planting. "Plant peanuts. That'll keep the soil productive. And the boll weevils don't attack peanuts," Carver said.[3] Aside from the dairy and planted fields, Grandpa kept other people's horses and mated his bull with their cattle.

"He [Grandpa] bought some land where there was a field near a river with a ditch for irrigation. It was the last house on the street and far apart from other homes. We kept horses for people and charged them for storage. The horses and cows would graze every day."

—UNCLE ANGUS

Grandpa's neighbors watched as he hand-dug a ditch along the edge of his land to siphon water at a tributary from the Red River to irrigate his crops and protect his house on a hill to avoid the "high water" of the rainy season. Grandpa and Grandma seemed to follow Tuskegee Institute's President Booker T. Washington's plans for Blacks in the post-Reconstruction years following enslavement and his insistence on gaining an education and becoming entrepreneurs through land ownership. How could he do this? It wasn't straightforward, and he was complex. The first thing that comes to mind when I think of Washington is Paul Laurence Dunbar's poem "We Wear the Mask."[4]

"We Wear the Mask"

We wear the mask that grins and lies,
It hides our cheeks and shades our eyes,—
This debt we pay to human guile;
With torn and bleeding hearts, we smile,
And mouth with myriad subtleties.

Why should the world be over-wise,
In counting all our tears and sighs?
Nay, let them only see us, while
    We wear the mask.

We smile, but, O great Christ, our cries
To thee from tortured souls arise.
We sing, but oh the clay is vile

Beneath our feet, and long the mile;
But let the world dream otherwise,
We wear the mask!

—Paul Laurence Dunbar

Washington developed a curriculum around what was necessary to run and sustain a thriving university town, and other historically Black colleges and universities embraced his model. His students, formerly enslaved people, had little to support themselves and their families after freedom came. Therefore, many agreed to sharecrop on land often owned by the former plantation owners who had enslaved them. It was a system that kept Black free persons under the yoke of a master, much like the slavery system.

Tailoring, sewing, weaving classes, and mattress-making offered women and men know-how in working with textiles and to gain skills for higher-paying jobs in the fast-growing industrialized workforce. Additionally, gardening, canning, and farming sustained the college community with food. There were also more creative courses in photography and wallpaper design. Washington recognized the skills and limitations within his student body and, through engaged learning and committed teachers, worked to balance intellectualism and practical education with his Head, Hand, and Heart approach.

Students came to Tuskegee with skills practiced on plantations, which in many cases were self-sustaining places, like micro towns with unpaid labor. Many formerly enslaved and their descendants who remained in the South chose the profession of a farmer because of skills before and during enslavement and after Reconstruction. To them, Washington encouraged land ownership. Becoming a farmer was a challenging profession. Yes, it provided farmers a closeness to nature, the ability to work outside and take pride in walking their fields, letting the wind hit their faces, smelling the different aromas from their fields, and forming relationships with other living things, their animals, as well as a way to sustain their families. But most farmers were dry farmers, dependent on the whims of nature, the sudden hard rains, or the searing sun that ruined crops and livelihoods. Washington's "Tuskegee Machine" targeted that group and educated students in the industrial trades as well as animal husbandry, horticulture, chemistry, botany, reading, writing, and more, providing information on progressive farming techniques and aiding farmers' development by providing outreach to their communities. His overarching goal was developing Black entrepreneurs through landownership, be it a farm or other type of property.

Washington founded the National Negro Business League (NNBL) in Boston, Massachusetts, in 1900. In 1899, W. E. B. Du Bois first had the idea of placing an NNBL "in every town and hamlet" where Blacks lived, but he didn't have enough financial backing to actualize his plan.[5] However, the strategically savvy Booker T. Washington, with his wealthy White financial backers, followed through with the goal. He visited Black businesses nationwide, observed their struggles, noted that banks denied them loans, and concluded that they needed a league to enable the business owners to work together on their behalf. Washington wanted the group to be political and thought wealthy Black leaders could collectively benefit in many areas of American life. "He brought Black business leaders together for mutual co-operation and trade advancement."[6] He also called for every business to represent Black men and women. Washington and Black dignitaries throughout Louisiana visited Southern University and A&M College in 1915 to encourage support and membership for the NNBL.

Unfortunately, Washington died the same year, and this may have been one of his last trips supporting his vision. The Shreveport chapter of the NNBL, founded in 1924, was part of the network established by Washington to increase economic development and support Black businesses in communities across the South. An article in the *Shreveport Sun* commented, "We have some professional and businessmen who state that they (Negroes themselves) have no confidence in the Negro, do not believe that a business league can amount to anything and by work and actions [discourage] others. Shreveport will never be what it should be if it follows the sentiment expressed by such men—progress is built on the optimist, not the pessimist."[7]

After Washington died, Robert R. Moton succeeded him as president of Tuskegee and leader of the NNBL. He sent George Washington Carver to a Farmers' Conference at Southern University and A&M College in 1918. Dr. Carver met with farmers to promote the safeguards of crop rotation for growing cotton and vegetables. These visits from Washington and Carver illustrate Tuskegee's influence on farmers. Many farmers were like Washington, born during the legacy of enslavement.

Although he was educated, many of the formerly enslaved who became farmers were not. His voice spoke to people where they were, "lifting them as we climbed," to quote Mary Church Terrell. Then, on June 6, 1933, President Franklin Delano Roosevelt signed the Credit Act, which improved federal lending to farmers.[8] It was mainly a game changer for Black farmers who were denied commercial credit from banks. Since it regulated loans at long last, Grandpa could file for the program for a loan. In 1934, he borrowed ninety dollars and paid it back before he died in 1935. If the funding had been available earlier, it could have strengthened his dairy business to be more prosperous and his health less strained. But that was not the case. My aunts and mother often spoke of his difficulties dealing with White inspectors and bank denials. The leaders from Tuskegee continued to lead and advocate for the Black business organization, especially farmers, even after 1945, when the office moved to Washington, DC. NNBL's mission continues to encourage Black business leaders and youth to become entrepreneurs.

"We'd drive the wagon around, and customers would bring a bowl to our wagon, and we'd pour the clabber milk cheese into their bowl and pour real sour cream on top of the cheese from our mold. Papa was very enterprising. There was not much competition because we took care of our customers—not too many Black families bought our dairy products because they didn't have the money to pay for them."
—UNCLE ANGUS

Businesses like the dairy distributed trade tokens, like the one pictured, from Lakeside Dairy to families to purchase goods. Perhaps my grandparents learned about helping communities access food and other goods from the NNBL organization and were probably members. Washington's overarching ideology, a belief in training "heads, hearts, and hands," ran hand in hand with their belief in "lifting as we climb." His influence on farmers through the Black extension agent system headed by his assistant, Thomas M. Campbell, head of the Negro Cooperative Service, proved paramount in creating a path that encouraged self-sufficiency among Black farmers. Grandpa hired several workers to help on the dairy until the boys, uncles David, Angus, and Booker, turned thirteen. He often provided boarding for his help.

A 10-cent trade token from Lakeside Dairy to purchase milk products.
Front: Lakeside Dairy, Angus Bates, Prop. Back: Good for 10c in Trade.

"There were four employees at the dairy besides the family. When me and Booker came of age, we took over the duties for the two guys, and dad let the two employees go as we took over. I was around thirteen. Booker and I weren't paid per se, but we always had spending money when we wanted something. At thirteen years old, we did all the chores. Our family dairy barn was concrete, with a refrigerator with sliding doors. Booker and I were milking about twenty-five cows at that time. We'd milk those and bring the rest of the cows and milk those. Booker would have to clean out the stalls and take the manure to the manure pile—all before school. When we got to the last three, I started chilling the milk. After filling the glass containers and chilling the milk, we'd get the milk out and load it up on the wagon with a refrigerator made for us by a blacksmith that kept the milk cold. We had a horse to pull the wagon, like the Kraft Cheese wagon. After it was loaded, all my dad had to do was drive away and deliver the milk. Sometimes I'd deliver the milk in the summer after school. I knew the route and I'd collect the money from the customers and give it to my mother. Mother was the bookkeeper. She gave us money to buy supplies—feed, hay, and tools, whatever it took."

—UNCLE ANGUS

Before working at the dairy, the children went to school and did fewer chores around the dairy. However, their parents understood the value and necessity of education for their children. So, while Grandpa didn't

Hired hands, Alonzo Edwards, Bud Lias, and Sam Ricks.

push too hard for his children to become immersed solely in the dairy business, he needed the boys to rise at three in the morning to do their dairy chores before going to school.

"We had milk in glass bottles, quarts, pints, and half pints. Only glass bottles. And we'd have to fill them by hand, and there were always two or three men working for our father."
—AUNT LIZZETTA

Many Black entrepreneurs in the South also followed Washington's lead and migrated across the country. They opened businesses and built communities, ensuring a wave of Black entrepreneurship. Besides Lakeside Dairy, the Allendale community boasted other Black companies, including two Black pharmacies for the whole of Shreveport at the time. The Bates family patronized other Black businesses like Dr. Powell, the family physician, who in 1928 was elected as the president of the local medical association, and Dr. Johnson, the family dentist, who was chosen as its secretary the same year. I also thought of Caesar Carpentier "C. C." Antoine (1836–1921), who served as lieutenant governor of Louisiana from 1873 to 1877 during Reconstruction.[9] He was their neighbor, living just a few blocks away. Born free in New Orleans, he governed during a brief period when those of African descent held power before the Compromise of 1877, which saw a racist US president installed who sided with the South in dismantling Reconstruction and, in its place, instituting the devastating and oppressive Jim Crow Era.

With the compromise ending his political ambitions, Antoine returned to life as a businessman, living part of the time at his Perrin Street home, built in 1905, two years before my grandpa built his house and dairy in the same neighborhood. Antoine was already successful, growing his businesses to include a grocery business and becoming partners in a cotton business and a cotton plantation in Caddo Parish. In addition to managing a thriving grocery business, Antoine partnered with former Black governor Pinckney Benton Stewart Pinchback in a New Orleans cotton factory business and real estate speculation in the Allendale district. He was also president of Cosmopolitan Life Insurance Company of Louisiana.

I thought about Antoine, a prosperous businessperson who may have been one of my grandparents' customers. At age eighty-five, he died at his residence in 1921, a few blocks away. Although they had some Black patrons, Uncle Angus commented that the cost of their dairy products was prohibitive for most Black households. Lakeside Dairy serviced other small companies that could be reached by old Bert pulling the milk wagon.

Historically, Louisiana is a complex state of many cultures due to its location along the Gulf of Mexico. French and Creole influences filtered into central and northern Louisiana, and cultural lines blurred between African Creole and Black Americans. Throughout Louisiana, at the beginning of the twentieth century, a large wave of Sicilians from Italy settled mainly in rural communities and then cities like Shreveport to start small businesses. Italian grocers opened a significant number of companies in downtown Shreveport. Although initially, many worked alongside Blacks in the fields, as non-Black people, opportunities opened for them to pursue businesses. Those opportunities opened up for Jewish merchants who settled in Shreveport, too. Still, Blacks had few opportunities to prosper. According to my mom and her siblings, these two immigrant groups were the primary business customers for Lakeside Dairy products, as White Southerners did not purchase the dairy products.

"The White folks wouldn't buy from Papa. He sold his milk to the Italians and Jews."
—MOM

"At that time, we didn't know Jews from Whites. We would sell milk to the Italian grocer, who was Dad's biggest customer. The grocery stores we delivered to sold our milk and dairy [products], and we would buy groceries from them."
—UNCLE ANGUS

Most people in Shreveport knew and liked Grandpa as a recognizable community member, as mentioned in the *Shreveport Sun* newspaper in the Ballyhoo section among the "many friends we see in everyday life" section. Once finishing his milk rounds, he sometimes stopped and socialized with friends, staying too long for Bert, his mule.

"My dad would stop somewhere to get a 'tightener' (a nip). If he stayed too long, the mule would return home with the wagon, but it never had an accident. It would stand in the driveway until someone unloaded the bottles from the wagon."
—UNCLE ANGUS

"Papa had an old mule named Bert who had more sense than a man. He knew how to open the gate, leave, and come back before Papa came back from delivering milk."
—COUSIN ANITA, AUNT BEAUT'S (JANICE) DAUGHTER

Texas Avenue, a commercial district Blacks called "The Avenue," was the Black business district. It boasted doctors, dentists, a pharmacy, a newspaper, barbers, a shaving parlor, and a notary public. Texas Avenue was a commercial destination for African Americans in Shreveport, referred to simply as "The Avenue." At the same time, a mixed residential and business district on the other side of Allendale, the St. Paul's Bottoms, also called Ledbetter Heights, had turned into a Black neighborhood. Renamed Ledbetter Heights in honor of renowned blues singer Huddie Ledbetter, the area, including Sprague Street, was an African American social entertainment district in the 1940s and 1950s. Before the civil rights movement, the Castle Hotel on Sprague Street was one of the only Black-owned hotels that served visitors and famous African American celebrities. The Castle Hotel and the Bottoms, close to the nearby Municipal Auditorium, made the Municipal a trendy venue for Black entertainers in the 1960s and 1970s. In the 1880s, the buildings were rental housing for Blacks transitioning from rural to urban jobs. The National Historic Register added St. Paul's Bottoms as a Historic District in 1999. Lebanese, Jewish, Italian, and Chinese businesses occupied other buildings on the block. Immigrants and Blacks living in the same neighborhoods were a reality in other parts of Louisiana during the early twentieth century.

Aside from the dairy, Grandpa maintained his fields by planting peanuts to enrich the soil for the oncoming spring season. Now, in the fall again, they were ready for harvesting. Once gathered, Grandma saved them in croaker sacks under the house near the potatoes, and as the weather turned cold, the boys pulled them out and roasted them for a protein-filled snack. Grandma and her daughters canned fruits and vegetables in sparkling-clean glass jars.

"A variety of trees had been planted around our house long ago: one apple, two pears, one quince, two plums, one peach, two figs, and two pecans and one walnut tree."
—UNCLE ANGUS

At Lakeside Dairy, the family planted seeds for turnip, collard, mustard greens, cabbage, and onions in early fall. They gathered leftover corn kernels for the cows and other farm animals for the winter and dug up the remaining sweet and Irish potatoes. Grandpa ensured he had enough hayseeds to yield a blonde summer carpet—ready to cut. The fall harvest would feed the cows during the winter until they returned to grazing on spring's promise of new grass shoots. Grandpa always had to buy extra hay to feed the animals on cold winter nights.

"We all helped. I washed the dishes, cleaned the bathroom, helped with the smaller siblings, and any of the household chores. There were trees around, so we had to rake leaves to keep the front yard clean. If the hired men didn't show up for work, we would have to help washing milk bottles and help clean the barn."

—AUNT LILLY

Home demonstration agents encouraged farmers to reroute waters from heavy rain to avoid flooding and evaluated their agricultural terracing to protect their crops and pastures where their livestock roamed. They recommended planting grasses to protect potential wind and water erosion from washing away their topsoil. Although I write down passages from family conversations about the dairy, my twenty-first-century mind cannot ignore Black people's status in Louisiana and their living conditions. Although lush and green, rural, and pastoral, the Southern environments had dangers in the soil and waterways from overuse of herbicide sprays and toxic run-off from the logging industry. But in northern Louisiana, rich oil and gas companies extracted mineral and oil deposits from many neighborhoods, including Black ones. Oil and gas discoveries in the 1870s helped heat and warm homes in Shreveport with electricity. As it turned out, many of the oil and gas deposits were on the land of Black families who sold mineral rights to speculators for pennies on a dollar. Once the oil and gas wells ran dry, many wells were not correctly plugged, and they continually leaked toxic substances like methane gas, which contains the cancer-causing chemical benzene.[10]

Historically, Blacks could purchase land parcels that Whites did not want: the leftovers. Being Black and wanting to own land meant accepting these conditions or having nothing. Grandpa knew what he was working with, so he organized his dairy farm to grow his vegetables near the house and hay in a field opposite where the cows grazed. He used the dried cow manure from the dairy and chicken manure in the vegetable garden of turnips, leafy greens, and flowers. Nothing was grown where the suspected sewage pipe emptied into the lake. Pollution sources from pasturelands were a problem for water quality in Louisiana, as it was in many parts of the country.

"There was a big black sewage pipe, and we'd walk along the pipe to gather the cows from grazing and bring them back home. The dog's name was Red. He'd round the cows up and make them cross the ditch and come home. We didn't have to worry about anyone. We bred the bull to the other cows in the community and charged three dollars per breeding session. The owner would bring the cows to our barn in the morning, the bull would mate with the cows, and owners would return for their cows that evening. They'd mate and then it'd be time for her to go back home. We kept horses for people for one dollar per day."

—UNCLE ANGUS

Fish and wildlife propagation has long been an issue for Louisiana's waterways. The Red River poured into Cross Lake at the edge of the dairy, sometimes carrying hazardous chemicals from the pulpwood operations. Many Black men worked in the lumberyards, which employed more Blacks than any other industry in Louisiana and other states with thriving sawmill communities. Work there proved similarly dangerous to jobs in agriculture plantations growing tobacco, sugar cane, and cotton.[11]

I now understand why farmers were encouraged not to cut the wildflowers from the sides of roads for their houses because of contamination. At the dairy, digging ditches around the fenced cow pins stopped the waste from running into the vegetable garden. Grandpa took as many precautions as he could to stave off pollutants. Thinking of Grandpa, it must have been challenging for a Black man going into the dairy business in 1907. As producers of premium-grade raw milk, especially before pasteurization, cleanliness was the rule on the farm, and all family members worked their chosen jobs to keep the dairy, its cows, and equipment clean and free of bacteria. That was the primary task of the children, and they had other chores, too. They knew that the grounds reflected their pride of place, which Booker T. Washington stressed for all entrepreneurs.

"The dairy consisted of Jersey cows and two or three host teams (breeds inferior to Jersey). The rich milk comes from the Jerseys, and 'filler' milk comes from the host team. It was Grade A milk

certified by the City of Shreveport. The inspector would get into
the milk wagon and inspect two or three bottles of milk and let
you know what condition the milk was in. Sometimes, they would
catch us along the route and take two or three bottles and take
them to the city for inspection."

—UNCLE ANGUS

"It was twelve of us [children] living in the house at the same
time. He [Grandpa] had a lot of mouths to feed and was very
prosperous."

—UNCLE ANGUS

Grandma, a tall, lean woman with a house full of children, rarely
wore her long hair down. Birthing twelve children, it seemed as though
she was always pregnant. Grandma loved her family, but her pensive
face showed the strain of caring for many. She kept their health in
check—her children visited the doctor and dentists regularly, got their
shots, and were always presentable in clean, crisp, ironed clothing and
shined shoes. Grandma kept a financial ledger on dairy operations,
insurance records, and the family's benevolent society contributions.
But, in all my ruffling through family photographs, I have not found
any pictures of her smiling.

According to the 1910 census, Grandpa and Grandma could read,
and she became the perfect partner to relay the latest farming methods
to Grandpa. Communities of Black farmers and their wives kept informed about Carver's brochures on crops, cultivation techniques, and
recipes for nutritious meals; another vital source of information was
the Tuskegee Institute's bi-weekly paper, *The Negro Farmer*.

Also, the women who could read followed Carver's suggestions, grew
flowers in their vegetable gardens, and picked wildflowers from the fields
to brighten the houses' interiors. Black American women's gardens
seemed chaotic and disarrayed like their quilts. But they willfully took
liberties with uniformity and symmetry, mingling their creative sensibil-
ity with functionality and use. Grandma arranged fresh flowers to bring
beauty into her home as a Golden Star Art Club member. Grandma also
seemed to appreciate the beauty in her natural surroundings and was
perhaps delighted to know about Carver's walks in the woods at a young
age and the flowers he'd find growing at the feet of trees.

Grandma, Carrie Davis Bates near the chicken yard.

Grandma's generation expected much of women on a farm besides caring for children and tending the domestic space, including a house garden. She raised chickens for eggs and dried and canned fruits, such as berries, plums, peaches, and apples, to sell. She took charge of her own space on the dairy, intuitively cultivating a garden of mixed vegetables, a favorite sweet pea, and aster flowers. But she also planted strong-smelling marigolds and herbs that her mother said helped protect her vegetables and other flowers from pests. She sold vegetables and flowers from her garden space and fruits from the trees planted around the house, developing a cottage enterprise from her home.

Aunt Lula was no doubt influenced by her mother's flower garden. Grandma and her children beautified the property along the fence that enclosed the front yard by transplanting flowers like wild roses, morning glory vines, dogwood trees, or shrubs from the woodlands. In Louisiana, families also passed along planting techniques used by the captured and enslaved, who were often the gardeners on plantations.

Aunt Lula standing in front of the fig tree and rose garden,
the domain of her mother.

As hard times during the depression increased, the children's chores increased, too. All of them, including the girls, had to pitch in and help wash the tin milk jugs and clear glass bottles, feed the cows and other animals, clean the barn, and do any outside chores at the dairy. While the men usually tended the dairy operation, livestock, and cash crops in the fields, Grandma and the girls recorded the financials. They helped their mother keep the budget and distribution of payments to vendors for supplies and other implements to keep the dairy running smoothly. The couple were frugal savers, keeping an eye on sustaining their family long-term.

"The hardest time was probably during the depression and after my father died. Our needs were always met before then: food, clothes, etc., and a roof over our heads. Less income made it more difficult to live. My father kept a Christmas Savings Club for us each year. At Christmastime, we would get our Christmas Saving—the amount of $12.50. It was one thing I always remembered to try and save a little money. After I had grown up, I always kept Christmas Savings, and I do until this day."

—MOM

But as partners in the success of the dairy operation, roles often shifted when the dairy called for all hands during planting, harvest, and getting their milk, produce, and livestock to market. Grandma and the girls cut vegetables like okra into bite-sized pieces and blanched them for thickening soups. Then, they canned them in glass jars to pull out on cold winter days. Grandma oversaw all the growing and harvesting of the kitchen vegetables and fruits. As a progressive woman, she knew that she had an equal stake in the success of Lakeside Dairy.

"She gave us money to buy supplies, feed, hay, and tools. We bought hay, forty to fifty loads of hay from Kambeck and Burkett Feed House. It came in hundred-pound sacks. The relationships were good with our vendors. We paid cash money for everything. Green spoke volumes. It was the color of the relationship. We collected cash money for the dairy once a week. If people couldn't pay, we never delivered to them again."

—UNCLE ANGUS

Even at the chilling end of fall, all activity continued its life cycle under the topsoil. The germinating seeds underground rewarded the family with tender grass sprouts for their cattle in the spring. But, at Lakeside Dairy, the first chill in the autumn air meant winter was coming.

"[We] would go out in the woods and cut our own Christmas tree. I still have the recipe for the Christmas nut cake, which had been in the family for years."

—AUNT LILLY

"At Christmas the adults would go out and cut down a tree for our living room. We would decorate the tree and wrap and put presents underneath. It was a festive time of year."

—ELOISE

"Dad would buy bacon and a whole ham. He'd buy three to four chickens at Thanksgiving and Christmas. We would have a turkey, dressing, and all kinds of vegetables from the garden. The desserts I remembered were cakes and pies. The most memorable were sweet potato pie, coconut cake, and pineapple cake."

—UNCLE ANGUS

But my mother remembers roast duck as the centerpiece of all their holiday meals. Furthermore, she remembers holidays celebrated in a different order than we currently celebrate them.

"We would celebrate all the holidays like this—Christmas, Thanksgiving, and Easter."

—ELOISE

Annual celebrations of harvests spanning different cultures occur between August and December. For the Bates family, Thanksgiving was an end-of-the-year celebration, but like the traditional US Thanksgiving, it included wildfowl, in their case, duck, and plenty of vegetables. This was not Kwanza, an American pan-African-inspired harvest developed by Maulana Karenga, a Long Beach State University professor, in 1966. The Bateses' harvest celebration preceded Karenga's by decades, and I am not sure why they celebrated after Christmas.

TWO FAMILIES UNKNOWINGLY CROSS PATHS

Both the Bateses and the Leffalls, my father's family, share similar stories of how their families settled in northwest Louisiana and northeast Texas. Although aspects of the stories differ, enslavers outrunning the Union Army brought their human property to Louisiana and Texas. Great-Grandma Bates came from North Carolina, and Great-Grandpa Leffall came from Georgia. The first groups of enslaved persons made East Texas the largest concentration of enslaved Black people in the state. By 1850, planter families in Harrison County had more Black enslaved people than any other county in Texas because those plantation owners in the Deep South sent their enslaved persons to Louisiana, Arkansas, and Texas. They did this to maintain their ownership of the

Great-Grandpa Jackson "Jack" Andrew Leffall is a cotton farmer.

enslaved as the Union Army marched and won battles and freed the enslaved populations until the end of the Civil War. Although Texas and Louisiana landowners found ways of securing the labor of their Black freedmen, many walked away as free people once they earned enough money to purchase their own land.

In many instances, Black farmers bought land located near former plantations where they were enslaved.[12] During Reconstruction, it appears when purchasing land and becoming a businessperson, mulattos had a distinct advantage before the Compromise of 1877. Even after the Compromise, the dye was set, and skin color often remained a determining factor for privileges and opportunities. According to relatives on both sides of my family, Black farmers who owned their land sold their products in the primary market in Shreveport. This led me to wonder if Grandfather Bates and Great-Grandfather Leffall knew each other.

Great-Grandpa Jackson "Jack" Andrew Leffall lived in Elysian Fields near Marshall, Texas. Although older, he was still a business contemporary of my mother's father, Angus Bates. J. M. Furrah, a major landowner who grew cotton and had a general store in Old Elysian Fields, enslaved Jack before freedom came. When freed, Jack continued to work in Furrah's fields for pay. Formerly enslaved people could share crops on Furrah's plantation, work crops, and receive a share of the harvest. After working for the J. M. Furrah family and learning about the cotton business, Jack purchased land from Furrah in 1910.

"Jack promised that if he were allowed to make money if he would make a dime, he would save a nickel. His ultimate goal was to buy his own land one day."
—BERDIE LEFFALL PIERCE

So, in some cases, Blacks obtained land through their working relationship with slave-holding planters, and Jackson purchased land for planting and growing cotton from that family. The large cotton plantations depleted the land. Because he did business in Shreveport, he would have learned about George Washington Carver's efforts to encourage Black farmers in Louisiana to plant rotating crops. But he only knew how to grow cotton, and Shreveport was the primary market for it. Small and large cotton growers alike offloaded their cotton crops in Shreveport. I don't know how many Black businesspeople were in Shreveport then, but it is highly likely that the dairyman Angus Bates and the cotton grower, Great-Grandpa "Jack" Leffall, crossed paths. Grandpa Bates had clients all over Shreveport and sold his milk products to businesses and anyone willing to pay. Decades after Jackson Leffall, Grandpa's ability to purchase land followed a similar practice of buying land from a former slaveholder, except he was probably a White relative.

Great-Grandpa Jack and the other Leffalls settled in an area called Pleasant Valley in the community of Old Elysian Fields east of Marshall. In 1885, Harrison County approved a four-acre parcel of land: three specifically to build Mount Pleasant Church and one acre for a school. Jack Leffall was one of the deacon representatives who contributed money for the $150 purchase from George and Myra Bishop. The deed filed in

1919 shows his name. Before Jack purchased his property in 1910, the town of Elysian Fields moved east, closer to the larger city of Marshall, to take advantage of tracks laid by the East Texas Railway. As a result, the new town grew and prospered. The Old Elysian Fields had few services, but Jack planted cotton in the sparsely populated landscape. He eventually owned 450 acres. Cotton, along with lumber, was one of the primary crops in East Texas. Black laborers made up the workforce in both sectors. The new railroad was the primary transportation method for getting cotton to market. But small farmers away from the tracks, like Great-Grandpa Jack, loaded cotton onto their horse-drawn wagons and drove it to Shreveport.

With the aid of family and harvesters, they quickly picked his cotton, gingerly pulling out the white fluffy cotton balls, fingers between the four sharp thorns, gently pulling the cotton away from its ball and dropping it into their bags. Some merchants wanted carefully picked clean cotton. Quality rather than quantity also garnered a higher grade. So, once baled, the slowly picked cotton was packed on his wagon and driven to discerning buyers in Shreveport.

Jackson Leffall might have encountered other members of the Bates family, like uncles Angus, Booker T, or David, a Waskom dairyman. He followed in his father's footsteps, taking his milk products in a refrigerated truck to clients in the more profitable Shreveport. Some of the same client families patronized his father and mother when they owned Lakeside Dairy and Carrie D. Bates and Sons Dairy.

I had no idea I had a cotton grower in the family. I knew about the cotton growing area because my Uncle Booker used to sing the song "Old Cottonfields." While writing this passage in my book, the words of Huddie "Lead Belly" Ledbetter, who was born in Louisiana and grew up in the same area as the Leffalls in Harrison County, Texas, rang out in my head. "It was down in Louisiana, just about a mile from Texarkana, in those old cotton fields back home," he sang. Growing up in Los Angeles, I heard my Uncle Booker T walking down the street singing passages from blues songs, and this was one of them.

I mentioned Elysian Fields to my second cousin, Shonda, who grew up in Shreveport near her grandmother, my Aunt Beaut, in the 1950s and 1960s. She remembered going to Elysian Fields as a child, saying it was nothing but country.

"It was awful. I mean outhouses, awful."
—COUSIN SHONDA

Since the Leffalls still owned much of Great-Grandpa Jack's land in Elysian Fields near Marshall, some left California and returned to their family seat. But after the Bateses left the pasturelands and the site of Lakeside Dairy, when Grandma passed, the family sold the house and land because no one was interested in returning.

Collard Greens.

COLLARD GREENS

Collard greens were one of our staple vegetables growing up in Los Angeles, as they were for the Bates family in Shreveport. As an adult, I continued planting collard greens in my garden as I moved from Los Angeles to Oakland, Portland, and Santa Rosa. They anchored my garden with a nod to my ancestors.

Hands-on time: 1 hour, 15 minutes
Total time: 1 hour, 15 minutes
Serves: 8–12

Ingredients:
  2 bunches of collard greens (washed and rinsed)
  1 tsp. salt (or to taste)
  1 tsp. black pepper (or to taste)
  2 tsp. Creole seasoning
  ½ bell pepper, chopped
  1 onion, thinly sliced
  2 stalks celery, diced
  2 cloves of garlic, thinly sliced
  1 tsp. vinegar
  1 cup chicken bone broth or stock
  2 tsp. paprika
  ½ cup water
  ½ cup raisins, optional
  ½ tsp. cinnamon, optional

Preparation:
  In a cast-iron pot over medium heat, sauté the trinity (onion, celery, bell pepper), fatback, or bacon if preferred, and seasonings, stirring often. After washing collard green leaves, take like-sizes, layer them, and roll them together like a paper roll. Holding the roll with one hand, chop it into ¼ inch sections and repeat for all the greens. Add collard greens to the cast-iron pot. Begin with a fast cook on high heat for 15 minutes. Reduce heat to a low-medium flame, and cook for 30–40 min on a medium flame, adding water and salt as needed to taste. Add cinnamon and raisins, if desired. Do not overcook. Greens should be tender but not overly limp. Keep adding water and seasonings if you want a savory pot "likker."

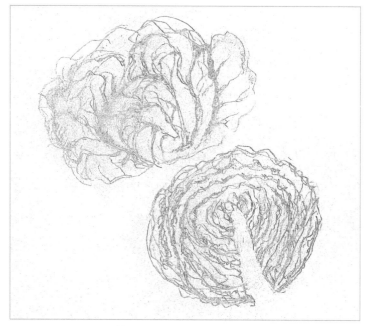

Cabbage and Carrots. Illustration by author.

CABBAGE AND CARROTS

We ate cabbage and carrots more often than greens for one simple reason: It was cheaper. I remember Mom chopping the carrots and sometimes we'd help her chop the carrots to go into the oversized simmering
pot. It seemed simple and ordinary but flavorful, especially with a hot
cornbread topped with butter. I'd break my cornbread into pieces in the
pot "likker" made from the cabbage and carrots and spoon up mouthfuls.

Hands-on time: 15 minutes
Total time: 20 minutes
Serves: 4

Ingredients:
    1 large head of green cabbage cut in half, then quartered, then cut
       each quarter into bite-pieces (about an inch)
    1 cup chicken stock or water
    1 cup carrots, chopped into ¼-inch rounds
    3 Tbsp. olive oil

1 onion, chopped
1 stalk of celery, diced
½ cup diced bell pepper
2 cloves garlic, chopped
1 Tbsp. apple cider vinegar
1 ham hock or turkey neck
Diced potatoes (optional)
1 Tbsp. butter
1 tsp. dried parsley
1 tsp. dried thyme
Salt and pepper to taste

Sauté the onion, bell pepper, carrots, and garlic in olive oil on medium heat until soft; add cabbage, ham hock/turkey neck, salt and pepper, potatoes (if using), and stock or water. Cook until the cabbage is limp but not soggy. Add butter and continue cooking for 5–10 minutes.

CARROTS AND TURNIPS

A variation on this recipe is carrots and turnips. When Mom often cooked turnip greens, she included the turnip bottoms. But other times, she also purchased turnips to make mashed carrots and turnip bottoms. The recipe is like the cabbage and carrot dish, but she added a bit of sugar and butter aside from mashing the turnips and carrots together.

Chop up a trinity (onion, bell pepper, celery), and sauté. Add chicken or vegetable stock or water to the peas. Bring to a boil and add the trinity. This recipe also applies to red cabbage, a favorite of my Aunt Lilly. Serves: 6–8

Ingredients:
½ head of red cabbage cut into 1-inch pieces
1 chopped brown onion
2 celery stalks, chopped
½ large bell pepper, chopped
2 carrots, cut into thin rounds
2 large garlic cloves, sliced
2 tsp. dried parsley

Carrots and Turnips. Illustration by author.

2 tsp. dried thyme
1 ½ Tbsp. apple cider vinegar
salt and pepper to taste

Preparation:
Sauté onions, bell pepper, celery, and carrots in butter and olive oil on medium heat for 15–20 minutes. Then add sliced garlic cloves and stir. Add chopped red cabbage and toss all ingredients until coated with butter and oil. Add parsley, thyme, salt, and pepper. Add apple cider vinegar. Cook over medium heat for 15 minutes, then reduce to a simmer for another 20–25 minutes. Taste for tenderness and flavor. Serve with hot buttered cornbread.

Butter Beans (Lima Beans). Illustration by author.

BUTTER BEANS (LIMA BEANS)

About once a month, Daddy woke up and put on a pot of lima beans. You could smell the ham hock throughout our entire California bungalow. When we rose, the soft and glistening beans were ready to eat.

Hands-on time: 30 minutes
Total time: 4 hours
Serves: 6–8

Ingredients:

1 lb. bag of dry lima beans
1 yellow onion, chopped
1 bell pepper, chopped
1 stalk celery, diced
2 cloves garlic, sliced
3 ham hocks (optional)
2 Tbsp. butter

2 Tbsp. olive oil
salt and pepper, to taste
2 bay leaves
garlic powder
chicken stock
green onion for serving
parsley for serving
Louisiana hot sauce for serving
¼ tsp. paprika, optional

Preparation:
Wash and sort dried lima beans, then flash-cook them in boiling water. Melt butter in a pot and sauté onions, bell pepper, and celery. When soft, add garlic. Add chicken stock, black pepper, salt, and 2 bay leaves, then simmer for an hour. Cook the ham hocks in a separate pot of water for one hour. Then add ham hocks to lima beans. Finish off with green onion and parsley. Cook covered for 1.5 hours. Add hot sauce, sit low for an hour, simmer, and take bay leaves out. Check for doneness. Season to taste. Add paprika if using.

Chapter Four

WORKING THROUGH THE ICY WINTER DAYS AND NIGHTS

"It was so muddy when it rained. First, we tiptoed through the mud going to and from school. Then, at home, we took off our dirty shoes and lined them up on the porch before coming into the house. It was so much mud."

—MOM

The Louisiana landscape turned icy cold. Hard rain on the dark, naked tree branches made them snap as the water turned to icicles. Just before dusk, a gray fog settled over the pasture. Lights in the community of houses around the farm twinkled in the distant windows like captured stars. Ice crystals formed on windowpanes. Winter set in at the dairy with colder white days and clear nights. Angus and Booker T bedded the cows down at night in the barn on a hay-covered floor. They had to protect them from the chilling night winds so they could produce milk the following day. After milking, the cows roamed freely in a grove of trees that protected them from the icy winds.

"We kept the cows in the barn at night and let them out in the day to walk around, but not into pasture because they'd wander too far for their own good."

—UNCLE ANGUS

"One morning we couldn't get the bridle on the horse. So, Booker and I got to whipping the horse, punishing it for not being able to get the bridle onto it. Then we told my dad. Dad came down and rubbed all the welts we put on the horse with the switches, from the back of the horse to the front. Dad whipped our asses that morning good for whipping that horse. This was all before his work and our school. We knew our jobs and didn't have to be told more than once to do it."

—UNCLE ANGUS

"I really didn't get into trouble because we were raised to be obedient, well-behaved children. But my older sister, Lilly, recalled my mother giving us a warning, 'I'm going to tear your building down!' before going to get a peach tree switch for a good whipping."

—MOM

The rain seemed to fall in glassy sheets, and a coat of ice covered everything in its wake. The Allendale community expected starry cold nights until March, but people still wanted their milk. My uncles fed the cows, and the older children delivered dairy products before heading to school. Before these early morning chores, Grandma got up in the darkness to make her daily batch of biscuits. During hunting season, they'd have duck for breakfast, too. She made enough biscuits to last throughout the day. The family huddled around the fireplace, especially during the ice storms. The towering pine trees snapped like matchsticks, falling and crashing in the woods with a crackle as they hit other trees and finally thundered to the woodland floor. Grandpa cut down the trees near electrical lines, but sometimes, a wayward limb fell into the line that ran down the main road, blacking out the whole community for weeks. Each year, Cross Lake would overflow at the back edge of Lakeside Dairy and cover all the pasturelands.

"Our street was the last street—so close to the lake."

—MOM

There was little work in the fields. The cold weather kept the children inside for most of the winter, as the family took comfort from sitting in front of the cozy fireplace, where they took turns cracking pecans and walnuts from the trees around the front yard. They also shelled peanuts, which had been gathered from the field and stored under the house in burlap sacks. They had enough nuts to eat all winter. The ambient light

One of two barns in the back of Lakeside Dairy (closed).

from the golden fire in the soot-covered fireplace provided enough light to save on electricity and heating for the small room off the kitchen where the children did their homework while munching on an after-school snack of toast or buttered bread. But in the winter, they often substituted butter for peanut butter. They had a field of peanuts that Dr. Carver suggested as a sustainable, quick-to-grow crop that was affordable to most farmers. He created recipes for delicious tasting and nourishing peanut-based foods and distributed them to farming households. One of his bulletins, "How to Grow the Peanut and 101 Ways of Preparing it for Human Consumption," released in 1925, became one of his most famous and cherished food preparation handbooks.[1] There are different recipes for peanut soups, using them boiled or mashed or adding peanut butter to water or milk. It's a basic West African soup that enslaved people brought to the New World, and some families continued to prepare them according to their regional tastes.

CRAFTING IN THE WINTER MONTHS

It was time for Grandma to reach for the bag of scraps she added to each year. It's almost quilting time when families settle in from outside work to craft inside projects. She collected and worked with her colored and textured patches of cloth from old clothing, as she did when sorting out different vegetables for her stews and soup, mindful of the harmonizing adage Dr. Carver promoted in cooking, planting, and crafting. The pigments he mixed for painting and clothing dye from Alabama's clay soil

Aunt Alma Collins's strip quilt, Plaquemine and Zwolle, Louisiana.

in his laboratory at the Tuskegee Institute brought affordable color into the lives and décor of Black farming communities. He is best known for using sustainable vegetable matter with the local red clay soil to create colored pigments, including the rediscovery of the royal blue color of Egypt. Artists knew it as the bluest of blues. First found in Egypt, for years, painters sought to rediscover the recipe. I imagined Grandma and her ladies' groups reading one of Dr. Carver's brochures about blue and other color dyestuffs.[2] He encouraged experimentation with his pigments. However, I don't know if Grandma ever mixed the dyes and dyed fabric. Still, swatches of old, blue, worn-out dungarees or bib overalls often suited quilters because of the fabric's various blue hues, sturdiness, and weight. Blue seemed to be a preferred color among many quilters. Aunt Alma, my husband's aunt from Plaquemine, Louisiana, made a striking blue quilt with embroidery accents from men's trouser strips.

Dr. Carver embraced his life work holistically as a scientist, painter, developer of natural dyestuffs, and creative thinker. Grandma chose her colored quilt swatches, combined them, and laid them down as if seasoning a mixture of vegetables in a big, black cast-iron pot. She cooked many stews and used different ingredients to experiment with their colors in her cooking pots and patchwork quilts. She mixed the colors and designs in her quilts, but most were strips, approximately twelve-inch by two-inch pieces of cloth pieced together in monochrome, abstract patterns, or a mixture of small colored strips. They were like paintings, reminding me of what George Washington Carver said relating the colors in painting to cooking, "In painting, the artist attempts to produce pleasing effects through the proper blending of colors. The cook must blend her food in such a manner as to produce dishes, which are attractive. Harmony in food is just as important as creating harmony with colors."[3]

Canning and freezing vegetable soup mixtures preserved the fall harvest season into the winter months. They added the vegetables to the Irish and sweet potatoes that they overwintered under the house to make vegetable soups, sometimes adding beef or chicken. In some seasons, the winters seemed to linger. Venison rounded out the need for protein during the winter months, along with ducks if they were lucky. As the ice glistened on the pine needles, the cold wind sucked up the air, and the wet winter took hold. The younger Bates sons ended up hunting for blackbirds. They were small compared to ducks but still a petite, tasty treat. Blackbirds assembled outside in the snow around the barn, picking up the droppings of grain from the feed inside the barn to feed the cows and pigs. Although it was not like northern winters with heavy snow days, it was enough snow to collect and make snow ice cream, a specialty for old and young alike. People also bought more milk to make their batches of ice cream, so the family appreciated any revenue-generating projects during this dormant growing season.

This practice brings me to discussing ice cream and lactose intolerance of dairy products and Black people. Although many ads show Black people eating and enjoying ice cream, health and wellness journals point to eating ice cream as one of the causes of a litany of diseases among Black people. Because my mother's family was a purveyor of dairy products, I wanted to know how they fared in this conversation on ice cream, especially because a Black ice cream maker, Henry Floke (or Florke), according to US Census records of Kentucky, owned an ice cream saloon in 1870.[4] Recent studies suggest that although Black people have the highest rate of lactose intolerance, they are also one of the groups that consume high rates of ice cream. Some suggest their intolerance comes from an otherwise poor diet; they should drink more dairy products to remedy deficiencies. Other articles say the generalization is incorrect. Not all Black people are lactose intolerant.[5]

Few articles discuss Black people and ice cream consumption, but there exists a history of dissuading Black people from eating ice cream because of early segregated ice cream parlors. They cite Kentucky, Louisiana, and Alabama as states with the least ice cream consumption.

Although the consumption of ice cream has long been a favorite treat of older Black people living in the Black Belt of the South, that was not always the case because of accessibility and cost.[6] Most Black people were tenant or sharecropper farmers in the community where Lakeside Dairy operated. They did not own their land. And as my Uncle Angus stated, they could not afford Lakeside Dairy products. The medical journals that discuss lactose intolerance among Blacks do not address the historical reality that the "right to buy ice cream in any establishment didn't just occur in the 1960s"; the NAACP was fighting the same type of discrimination cases in 1914.[7]

My favorite Aunt Lizzetta loved her vanilla ice cream. She could eat a pint in one sitting and have no problem. Each time my mother or sisters, even my sons, visited her, she requested they bring her a half-gallon of Thrifty's vanilla ice cream. My other elderly aunts always had vanilla ice cream on hand when we visited, probably influenced by the availability of homemade ice cream at the dairy. Vanilla ice cream was my grandpa's favorite dessert.

Other cold-weather activities included collecting wood for the fireplace and tossing pinecones at one another. The brownness of the fields and the rest of the landscape added to a stillness around the dairyland. The peace yielded clarity absent during the tilling, planting, weeding, harvesting, and turning seasons of spring, summer, and fall. It was also a time for sewing new dresses for the girls. But Grandma wasn't the only one sewing.

"I've heard so many funny stories about how she [Aunt Alice] would get out of her farm chores by agreeing to make clothes for her siblings. Then they would do her chores for her."
—COUSIN MICHELLE FLOWERS-TAYLOR

But the tranquility of the winter was only interrupted when the boys took night rides on the hood of cars to go rabbit hunting and in the woods when they went searching for squirrels, something that both my husband and uncles remember. Those rabbit bits were sometimes added to vegetable soup mixtures. I remember my mother cutting vegetables from the market to make her soups. At Lakeside Dairy, they would take the leftover vegetables during harvest and cut them into small pieces to freeze. In reading Carver's recipes in one of his bulletins, I came across "Miscellaneous—Odds and Ends." Under that heading, Carver wrote, "A variety of dried soup mixtures can be made by saving finely shredded onion, carrots, sweet peppers, bits of celery, okra pods, string beans, very tender, cowpea bods, cabbage, rutabagas, green and ripe tomatoes, etc. Shred all together nicely, dry in sun or oven of the stove the same as for other dried fruit or vegetables."[8]

In addition to heating the home, the fireplace at the dairy home was where my grandparents loaded up the sweet potatoes and put the pan in the hot ash. Sometimes, they put the potatoes in the ash by themselves and covered them with hot coals for about two hours until they were soft, with the caramelizing sap bursting through the skin. Mom made sweet potato pone—a crustless, baked casserole—rather than potato pies because she was concerned about keeping her weight down. She preferred it to candied sweet potatoes because of its savory, spiced taste. Like my mother, I do not make pies or candied versions. I learned to make sweet potato pone from memory by watching her cook, but I didn't write down the recipes. This one is from Jessica Harris's *The Welcome Table*, which I read when writing an essay on James Baldwin and the painter Beauford Delaney; with a bit of tweaking, it comes closest to my mother's, with plenty of butter.

I know the Bates family grew fields of peanuts, but I found no recipes or mention of peanut soup in the family records. Because they ate "high on the hog" and had beef cattle, peanut soup was probably not a priority in their household. But peanut stew served as a base for adding beef, lamb, or chicken; those variations are common throughout the African Diaspora. It doesn't mean the Bateses did not eat peanuts as snacks and prepare them for candies, especially at Christmastime.

Sweet Potatoes. Illustration by author.

SWEET POTATOES AND APPLES

My mother baked sweet potatoes in their skins and combined them
with apples. Like her, I like to bake the whole potatoes in their skins
and mix them with spices and cooked apples.

Hands-on time: 15 minutes
Total time: 1 hour
Serves: 6 to 8

Ingredients:
   3–4 medium sweet potatoes
   3 medium apples
   6 Tbsp. salted butter, or to taste
   ½ tsp. cinnamon
   pinch of fresh ground nutmeg
   ¼ tsp. salt
   2 Tbsp. brown sugar
   2 tsp. fresh lemon juice
   2 Tbsp. water (or more, so apples do not stick to the pan)

Preparation:

Preheat the oven to 350°F. Grease the sweet potato skins with canola oil and place the potatoes on a cookie sheet so they do not touch. Bake them until the fork goes quickly through the potato, about 45 to 50 minutes. While baking the potatoes, peel and chop the apples. Heat and cook with water and 1 Tbsp. of butter until soft but not mushy. Remove the potatoes and carefully peel off the skins, put them in a pot, and add the remaining 5 Tbsp. of butter (or less), salt, spices, and softened apples; mix and mash them into a rough texture. Then add the brown sugar and fresh lemon juice. Heat the potato and apple mixture until fully warm.

CHRISTMAS NUT CAKE

At home in Los Angeles, mom always made fruit pies. She rarely baked a cake, except for our birthdays and Christmas. The Christmas Nut Cake was a favorite in my family, with several of my aunts baking it as a welcoming treat in their homes as family visited during the holiday season. I used at least three types of nuts because I liked my cake nutty, including pecans, walnuts, hazelnuts, Brazil nuts, and even macadamia nuts.

Because we had so many lemons, she baked an old-fashioned lemon pound cake with a lemon glaze, a family favorite. I remember hearing my father go into the kitchen and cut himself a piece of the cake to enjoy with a glass of milk while we were all supposed to be asleep. The following day, substantial sections of the cakes were gone.

Hands-on time: 20 minutes
Total time: 2 hours, 40 minutes
Serves: 12–14

Ingredients:
½ cup molasses
1 tsp. baking soda
2 cups pecans, chopped
2 cups walnuts, chopped
2 cups Brazil nuts, chopped
1 cup hazelnuts, chopped

4 ½ cups raisins, apricots, or cherries (dried)
3 ½ cups all-purpose flour, divided
1 Tbsp. cinnamon
½ tsp. ground ginger
½ tsp. ground cloves
1 ½ cups salted butter
2 cups light brown sugar
½ tsp. cardamom
zest from 1 orange
juice from ½ lemon
6 large eggs
½ cup bourbon

Preparation:

Preheat oven to 250°F. Liberally grease a straight side angel food cake pan on all sides with butter or canola oil. Line the bottom with parchment paper. Mix molasses and baking soda with a spoon. It will start to expand and become a caramel color. After it rises to a cup, set it aside. In a large bowl, combine pecans, walnuts, and dried fruit in ½ cup flour and set them aside. Whisk together ground cloves, cardamom, ginger, and cinnamon with 3 cups of flour. Set aside. Cream butter, oil, and brown sugar together until light and fluffy. Add eggs one at a time, beating well into the mixture. Add molasses and soda and mix well. Add flour gradually until mixed well. Add nuts and dried fruits and mix well, scraping the sides of the mixing bowl. Add bourbon, mix, and scrape the sides well.

Spoon the mixture into the lined pan with a large spoon and smooth evenly across the top. Bake for two hours—test for doneness with a long skewer or butter knife. The cake is done if it comes out clean, with a few crumbs. Take it out of the oven and let it rest for 20 minutes. Turn it onto a wire rack and let it cool completely before slicing. Once cooled, you can spoon more bourbon onto your cake every few days to keep the cake moist. Wrap it in aluminum foil to preserve the moisture and taste. If you have a tin cake pan with a lid, store it there, and it will last even longer.

SPRING PLANNING
FOR THE NEXT YEAR

THE BATES CHILDREN WATCHED FROST AS IT MELTED ON THE FARM'S rooftops and barns. When the last frosty days melted away, it was time to till the soil and plant the vegetable seeds that Grandpa got from farm demonstration agents. He practiced the technique of "pair crop," or crop rotation, growing crops near other plants to yield more per acre, ensuring healthy planting soil, and reducing the devastation from pests. It increased the production and sustainability of food crops for everyone, the family and farm animals alike. Indigenous peoples in the Americas also practiced crop rotation.

The children jumped up early to greet the sunrise as the weather warmed. They looked forward to the warm springs with moderate rain and springtime mornings with whiffs of fragrant magnolias floating in the humid air, signaling a new and promised day. Spring was a good season to make fluffy yeast rolls, always served at church brunches, and watch flowers' sleeping bulbs burst up from the ground. Growing flowers was another way Grandma mindfully made a space for herself at Lakeside Dairy.

A time of early dawns and late sunsets meant extended work hours at the dairy, in the fields, and in the garden. A temperate spring folded into a hot subtropical climate from morning until night. The hot white sun bathed the fields—drying them until the blessing of spring rain came with increasing humidity levels. Unfortunately, the downpour was often heavy, and a surprise hailstorm could damage tender plants in the spring and summer. The rains provided nourishment for plants and weeds alike, which meant just after the rains, while the soil was still wet, hands had to get out into the field and pull weeds lest they choke the valued seedlings. But Dr. Carver cautioned farmers that weeds were not necessarily bad; they also had their place on the table. In his October 1942 bulletin, he encouraged farmers and their families to forage for edible plants around their homes, pastures, roads, and woodlands to sustain them during World War II. Folks were unsure if the war would come to the US shores or if there would be shortages of foodstuffs. Before listing the wild greens and notes on their preparation, Carver quoted a Bible scripture: "And God said, Behold, I have given you every herb bearing seed, which is upon the face of all the earth, and every tree, in which is the fruit of a tree yielding seed; to you it shall be for meat."[1] In this Bulletin, Dr. Carver believed that enough wild greens growing on roadsides and fruits like wild plum trees could help small farmers with few resources sustain a balanced diet. He provides recipes for foods like dandelion greens, wild lettuce, chicory, sheep sorrel, and many others. He said appropriately seasoned cooks could use these ingredients to make delicious meals for their families. As it turned out, foraging for flowers and other herbs rich in vitamins and minerals was a worldwide tradition, with the scarcity of food during World War II. Foraging was a savior for many families. Also, before the advent of industrialized crops, gathering weeds and flowers provided alternative greens to combat the brutal heat that scorched domesticated crops that needed more rainfall than weeds. Carver even gave instructions for gathering and preparing chicory to stretch coffee. I remember many Louisianans favored the taste of coffee with chicory added. They could purchase it in the marketplace, or some made their coffee-infused chicory from its root. Carver advised them to peel the chicory roots first, dry (or roast) them in the sun (or oven), grind, and brew. Then, for a slight change in taste, add dandelion roots.[2]

These suggestions helped sustain families through lean times, especially those with less. My grandparents were aware of the economic privileges in their community.

"Honey, I'm tellin' you, you can say what you want. We were segregated, but honey, we had a rich heritage back then."
—AUNT LILLY

While Grandpa and Grandma had little time for anything but the dairy operation and their children's health and education, they still enjoyed a few social outlets. Grandma was involved in the community's affairs. As the children grew, her attention turned to providing opportunities for other women and their children through her women's social club meetings in the house's parlor. The parlor always looked like a picture in a painting, rarely used, with button-tucked upholstered high-back chairs and china cups and saucers that had belonged to her mother, which she set out for her missionary meetings. The children helped their mother prepare the delicacies like teacakes for her meetings.

The older children peeked in on the Mary Church Terrell Club (later renamed the National Association of Colored Women's Clubs, NACWC) meetings in the parlor room. These meetings were of utmost importance to the convergence of sophisticated ladies who did not forget the common good of the Allendale community. Grandma wouldn't have it any other way—education was strategic to their community's survival. Believing in this, Grandmother fought just as hard for her neighbors' children's welfare as her own. She followed the vision of Terrell, who said, "And so, lifting as we climb, onward and upward we go, struggling and striving, and hoping that the buds and blossoms of our desires will burst into glorious fruition ere long."[3] "Lifting as we climb" became the motto of the NACWC. It was in concert with W. E. B. Du Bois's 1903 "Talent Tenth" essay, which also encouraged Black college-trained men to devote themselves to uplifting and serving the problems of Black people of lesser means.[4] The theme of lifting was taught as early as Sunday school Bible lessons, Luke 12:48: "For unto whomever much is given, of him shall be much required." Later, as Du Bois's support among educated Blacks lessened, he worried aloud that the new Black middle class was experiencing difficulties sustaining the lives they had carved out for themselves before migrating. Their money focused less on the problems of those farthest down. But Grandma was probably also aware of the efforts of Mary Murray Washington, Booker T. Washington's third wife, who advocated for improving the sanitary conditions in homes of formerly enslaved Blacks in rural areas. Washington, a Fisk University graduate, was the Lady Principal in charge of supervising women students and supervising women faculty at Tuskegee. She wrote about domestic solutions for farmers' wives. Although her position seemed to run contrary to the higher education position of my grandmother's NACWC leader, Mary Church Terrell, they were after the same thing: uplifting a nation of formerly enslaved persons. Washington presided over the National Federation of Afro-American Women. She also co-founded the National Association of Colored Women and was elected president in 1912. She focused on improving the lives of the Southern disadvantaged and former enslaved Blacks in communities around Tuskegee. Washington believed that "there was one thing that transcended work, school, and church, and was always of paramount importance: the home." Emphasizing industrial training and practical housewifery fell short among many of Mary Church Terrell's women's groups. Still, Washington's position at Tuskegee offered first-hand knowledge of many students' conditions. She influenced women with her "Bath, Broom, and Bible" program that served to empower the next generation of students with her focus on improvement and uplift.[5] She also wrote and gave speeches to women on topical subjects that celebrated Black achievement, like her 1929 speech "Dr. George W. Carver, the Man Who Can Make 200 Products from the Peanut."[6] She wanted women to be as informed as their male counterparts.

But, in good and bad times, communities in the South knew that the impoverished and those with a bit more wealth lived a stone's throw away from each other. Therefore, as Washington encouraged, the community must rise together, not just the fortunate few. The good ladies in Grandma's club believed in the ideology that a well-rounded education, no matter how little, served as a great equalizer. Grandma was also a devout Christian and a member of Antioch Baptist Church in Shreveport, like her mother.

"On moving to Shreveport, Louisiana, in 1900, I joined the Antioch Baptist Church by letter in 1900. At this date I have been in the service 32 years. I was elected president of the Woman's Work of the above church, Dec. 2, 1904, serving them to Jan. 10, 1908. Owning to affliction, I tendered my resignation as president [1911], but I am still identified with that line of work. Christ wants women to go on mission for Him. The women were last at the cross and first at the tomb."
—GREAT-GRANDMOTHER LILLY DAISY MORRIS DAVIS

Antioch Baptist Church, Shreveport, Louisiana.

"I was brought up in [Antioch Baptist Church] in Shreveport. Honey, it had a big crystal chandelier that hung from the ceiling. Honey, that's Antioch Baptist Church. Honey, I'm tellin' you, stained glass windows, [with an] organ upstairs in the organ loft. Honey, it was beautiful inside and everybody, we had our own pews. I mean they were pews too. They weren't little benches. Had our own pews in that church."

—AUNT LILLY

Grandma followed in the footsteps of her mother's community service. In Great-Grandmother's brief autobiography, *Life Sketches*, printed by a local print shop, she wrote about her life, her mission to do good in her community, and her belief in God. An excerpt follows:

I, LILLY D. MORRIS, The daughter of John & Pheobie Morris was born at Landzene La., Desoto Paris, Feb. 20th, 1866. The reader of history knows that this was a dark period. My first school privileges were at Bethel Baptist Church.

The reader of history knows that this was a dark period. Our school term lasted three months, so that we would forget in the nine months of vacation whatever we learned in the three months at school. However, in spite of these disadvantage, from an early childhood I had an object in view, namely: to do something for the cause of Christ and the uplift of humanity. My mother & father were earnest Christians (Thanks to God for my mother's fireside training). Every Sunday morning, she started me out to Sunday School with my little bare feet and sun bonnet. She taught me not to be ashamed of my bare feet and sunbonnet; for said she, "'tis not the dress that makes the lady, but pride, good manners, obedience, charity, and virtue—these qualities she insisted made a lady." She constantly urged me to do my best in securing an education.

Life is a road, man is a wanderer, heaven is a home. Should any traveler young or old, chance to read these passages, the prayer of the writer is that her struggles may be to them encouragement and that the goal of your ambition may be obtained by perseverance and simple faith in God.

—*LIFE SKETCH*, LILLY D. M. DAVIS, LECTURER, AND HOME MISSION WORKER

The level of my great-grandmother's involvement amazes me. It seemed like she had a deadline to accomplish her life's work. It turned out that she did have a deadline. She suffered from an illness unknown to me, but one she hinted at in her *Life Sketch*, saying, "Owning to affliction, I tendered my resignation as president; but I am still in that line of work."

I knew Great-Grandma was born a year after the abolition of slavery in the US in Frierson in DeSoto Parish, where her parents had been enslaved people. But I couldn't find the plantation name during many years of searching. I looked up plantations in the area and found Land's End Plantation, but I had no references for that place. Instead, I had a fuzzy photograph of a large house in the distance that we thought might have been the plantation. But we were lost without a label and no family to identify it. Then, years later, I reread *Life Sketches*. I had been so intrigued by Great-Grandma's description of her life that I missed an essential clue to her birthplace. She told me at the very beginning of her story. She wrote, "The daughter of John & Pheobie Morris was born at Landzene La., Desoto Paris, Feb. 20th, 1866." With so many Spanish and French place names, I had overlooked the misspelling of Lands' End. "Landzene," phonetically, was Lands' End Plantation in Stonewall, DeSoto Parish.

CALENDAR

The Golden Star Art Club

❖ ❖

1921 = 1951-52

Golden Star Art Club, 1921–1951–52.

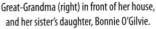

Great-Grandma (right) in front of her house,
and her sister's daughter, Bonnie O'Gilvie.

Since the nineteenth century, Black women wrote about their world, often about how women should conduct themselves. Whether they were of means or not, they should present themselves with dignity, humility, and grace. The social and church clubs empowered them to create pathways to participate in defining public policy in government, especially as it relates to women and their communities' welfare and health. Their social clubs actualized progressive agendas.

Great-Grandma Lilly embraced her clubs as part of her Christian duty. She was the president of her local Women's Work, Women's Home & Foreign Mission Society of the Women's Auxiliary to the National Convention, the Baptist Woman's Home Mission Society, and the Knights & Daughters of Tabor.

Like Great-Grandma, they created albums with poetry and sometimes artwork like flowers. They shared their albums and printed pamphlets and journals.

Grandma wasn't as active as her mother, but she joined the Knights & Daughters of Tabor, as her mother had, and the Golden Star Art Club, which encouraged and supported the arts in students' lives. The

The Knights & Daughters of Tabor.

Calendar for the club for the year 1951 lists the members. They mis-
spelled her name as Mrs. Angeles Bates rather than Mrs. Angus Bates.
She is listed as the hostess for meetings on January 9, 1951, and the
program head for January 1952 and May 1952. The programs at their
meetings promoted art appreciation in the visual arts, music, dance,
and literature.

A formerly enslaved person, Moses Dickson established the Black
fraternal organization, International Order of Twelve Knights and
Daughters of Tabor, in Independence, Missouri, in 1872. It was later
renamed the Golden Leaf Tab B 47. The Bates family belonged to the
group's local chapter. The Taborians sought to promote "Christianity,
education, morality and temperance and the art of governing, self-
reliance and true manhood and womanhood." While the organization
eventually had chapters across the United States, it flourished in the
South. This group is primarily known for its activities in Mississippi,
where it established the Taborian Hospital in Mound Bayou.[7]

With a broader readership among Black men and women, the Black
press fueled the development and kept information flowing into Black
communities. These papers shared information on politics, social

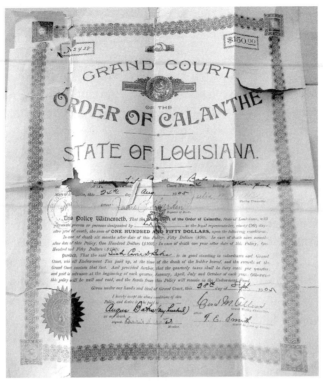

Grand Court of the Calanthe.

interactions, education, and the arts. Just as many women wrote and read poems at their social gatherings, they also read poetry printed in the pages of newspapers. For example, after John Willis Menard's unsuccessful seating as a Louisiana congressman, he left for Florida. While there, he took other government jobs, edited newspapers, and wrote a collection of poems, *Lays in Summer Lands*, published in 1879. This collection shows his awareness and embrace of the Atlantic Black diaspora and his sensitivity to people of African descent in the Americas and Caribbean. Although some poems are about the rough and tumble world of Reconstruction politics and the challenges of racism toward the formally enslaved, Menard also constructs imagery that connects people to their landscapes. *Lays in Summer Lands* is a fascinating collection of his poems because of Menard's consciousness of the Atlantic Black diaspora and his uncanny ability to connect people to the environment in which they live. Subjects such as the love of a woman, landscape, and a sense of place enliven our perception of the lives of

Creole and Black populations of the Atlantic Black diaspora. Images of freed persons also present visual contrasts to the everyday existence of Black populations in the Atlantic Black diaspora.

Although Menard later left Florida for Washington, DC, his poems mirror a landscape close to his heart. He found similarities between the geographies of eastern coastal Florida and the Gulf of Louisiana, seamlessly connecting them with other areas of the Caribbean diaspora. He did not write in a vacuum. He tied his romantic love for his second wife, Elizabeth, to that of tropical landscapes. After meeting her on an official trip to Jamaica, he fell in love and wrote to her after returning to the US, professing his love and languishing to be with her. His poems are more inclusive of the many cultures in the places where he lived than other writers of his day. Although his family boasted of their French Creole lineage, he was sensitive to the presence of diverse populations of Blacks. For work, he traveled internationally to Caribbean countries rich in Black cultural histories, like Jamaica, Honduras, Cuba, and Belize, which figure significantly in his life and writing. Menard saw a connection between the Black inhabitants of the Caribbean in his former home in New Orleans, his adopted homes in Jacksonville, and later Key West.

Teachers, writers, editors like Menard, and social organizations were cultural agents, uplifting people through literature and education, creating a sense of self-worth among their members that they transferred to the broader communities of Black people. Some groups spanned the highly educated to those with less education. However, when poorer Black women didn't belong to these organizations and clubs, they were still active as large and small change agents in their communities. Historically, their grassroots movements placed them on the front lines with the loudest voices for change. They championed better working conditions, education, housing, food and water security, and medical care. They taught and encouraged other women in sustainable ways of living. Community activism bolstered my grandmother, who caught the bus to take my cousin Bobby to the Shriner's hospital, insisting they correct his clubbed feet.

Grandpa accepted the clubs as part of his wife's civic duty, but he frowned at all the churchgoing and what he felt was the self-importance of the church and club ladies. But Grandpa also had his men's groups, which were more agreeable to him than church work. One of his clubs was shrouded in mystery and secret rituals that had something to do with calling on the ancestors who they felt guided and protected them and their families from Louisiana's socially and politically oppressive system. The Black secret societies that Grandpa joined provided members power in their organizations that they could not have in the broader multiracial community. Nevertheless, this all-male network founded a safe Black place where the community's men, mainly landowners and entrepreneurs, could talk and plan in the face of economic disenfranchisement. These organizations were essential in self-actualizing their freedom away from the oppressive racial realities in the South.

Aunt Lizzetta & Aunt Lilly's Teacakes.

AUNT LIZZETTA & AUNT LILLY'S TEACAKES

On our visits, Aunt Lizzetta (Los Angeles) and Aunt Lilly (San Francisco) treated us to teacakes. Aunt Lizzetta's teacakes were noteworthy for their almond taste, and Aunt Lilly's for their lemony flavor. The recipe below interprets the mixture of flavors that I remember from their flavorful treats. I liked both. Depending on my mood, I want crispy almond or lemony sweetened cakes. But I always combined flavors of almond and lemon in my memory in both. I also consulted with my sister, Deborah, and added her twist to this recipe.

Hands-on time: 20 minutes
Total time: 40 minutes
Yield: 24–30 tea cakes

Ingredients:
   3 ½ cup sifted all-purpose flour
   1 cup granulated sugar
   1 tsp. baking powder
   ½ tsp. salt
   ½ tsp. nutmeg
   ⅓ cup shortening or
   2 eggs beaten
   ¼ tsp. vanilla
   ½ tsp. almond extract
   ½ tsp. nutmeg
   1 tsp. lemon zest
   ½ cup buttermilk

Preparation:
   Grease baking sheets with lard or other oil. Preheat oven to 425°F.
   Sift flour with all other dry ingredients except sugar. Cream butter
   and sugar; mix until smooth and fluffy. Then add beaten eggs, vanilla,
   almond extract, and lemon zest and mix until combined. Alternate
   adding flour and buttermilk in 2 or 3 portions, beginning and ending with flour. Stir gently between additions until smooth. Put into
   a bowl in the refrigerator to chill. Remove 1/3 of the dough at a time
   to a floured pastry cloth and roll out about 1/4-inch thick. Sprinkle
   lightly with sugar. Cut with a 2-½-inch cookie cutter or rim of a
   drinking glass and lift with a spatula onto a baking sheet. Repeat with
   the remaining dough. Bake in the middle of the oven rack for 10–12
   minutes or until lightly brown around the edges. Remove from the
   baking sheet and cool on a rack.

Chapter Six

SUMMER GROWING, GATHERING, AND COOKING ON HOT AND LAZY DAYS

WEEDS WERE A SAVIOR WHEN THE HEAT WAS BRUTAL. THEY SEEMED to challenge the sun's searing rays when it ruined vegetable crops around them. When it rained, it was still hot. After the rain, the steamy heat increased the humidity so greatly that one could hardly breathe. Farmers had to get out into the fields or gardens before the sun rose. They worked with their backs bent, heads down, and hands into the earth until they cleaned all rows. As farmers weeded, the birds were right behind them, gathering up any insects that couldn't scurry back into the soil fast enough. At the dairy, life returned to the tasks at hand—the cornfields had provided fresh ears of corn for boiling on the cob, "roast 'nears," roasting the ears over an open fire, dried corn for popcorn or grinding for grits, or leftover corn treats for the cows, horses, pigs, and chickens, in that order. The farm animals also got treats and carrots.

There was still plenty of summer and crookneck squash, okra, tomatoes, and corn for succotash. The Bateses ate various fresh, farm-to-table vegetables, picking them early before the dew evaporated off their leaves. The menu depended on the ripeness of the offerings in the field and garden for that day. Whatever they combined, that African transplant, okra, was often in a savory mix of colorful vegetable morsels, usually fried in a black cast-iron skillet or used as a thickener for soups.

In Los Angeles, we ate succotash made of butter beans (lima beans), okra, corn, and tomatoes. Also raised in a northern Louisiana farming family, my husband remembers summers when his mother needed fresh butterbeans. He or his siblings picked them for preparation in succotash or other meals. In Los Angeles, fresh lima beans completed our family's modified succotash version of okra, corn, and tomato.

So, the siblings helped their parents on the dairy in the summertime, filled with lazy days and humid nights. The children brought their sheets and pillows onto the screened sleeping porch on those too-hot-to-sleep nights, trying to catch a breeze that wasn't there from the big willow tree in the front yard. On many days and nights, folks often commented: "You couldn't buy a breeze." But the humming sounds of crickets rubbing their hind legs filled the air, augmented by croaking frogs, a symphony that lulled the children to sleep in the night's heat. A dreamy moon watched over the children as they slept. Its luminous light drifted through their house's screened porch and windows, and all was well and safe again.

By late August, the long summer days were ending. The early morning sun lifted, parting the siblings' closed eyes. It was time for work before the heat's intensity hung over the field.

"I'm going to tell you when we washed. First, we put clothes on the stove in a kettle. Then we would take them out on the back porch, which had a large back. And that's where we would wash them in the tin tub. So, after we cleaned them, we transported them to where we would soak them in the tin tub. Then, after we got the bathtub on the other side of the kitchen, we filled it up with bluing water and rinsed all these clothes for a family of eight or nine. Then, after we finished washing and putting clothes on the line, which we had scrubbed on the rub board, we could swim in the bluing water in the bathtub. So then, we had two clotheslines, there were always clothes on the lines. And what we couldn't hang on the clothesline, we would lay on the fence going down the hill to the barn. And looking back on it, it was living."

—MOM

"If they started early, they could end the day soon and rest in the shadows of the afternoon, and besides, it was county fair time. Black people had to go [the] last day of the fair. Mama would take us, and I would watch the Ferris wheel. It would make me so dizzy. I couldn't do anything but stretch out on the grass. But we could only ride on the Ferris wheel on the Black Fair day."

—AUNT LILLY

At the end of summer, the heavy branches of peach and fig trees hung low, beckoning the children to pick the ripe orbs before they dropped to the ground. They had to pick them, or the birds and other critters would surely eat their hard-earned work with the trees. Apples ripened later in the fall. All the fruit was picked and packed into canning jars for the winter, with some peaches saved for peach cobbler. Then, it was raking time. With the turning leaves on the fruit and nut trees, the children knew that raking leaves and more leaves added to their usual chores to consume hours of their day. Their parents took pride in a clean and presentable home site, so the children's tasks were tidying up the grounds around the house and collecting fallen leaves and rotten fruit.

"There were trees, so we had to rake leaves to keep the front yard clean."

—MOM

Watermelons, which grew in abundance, were an end-of-summer treat. From the turn of the century, many upwardly mobile Blacks shunned the red melons because of the derogatory imagery of "darkies," especially little "pickaninnies" with broad grins and bulging eyes pictured with a piece of watermelon. Some Black people continued to avoid watermelon around White folks because of the negative portrayals of Black people eating the fruit. But many Black folks exerted their cultural agency by eating this national melon of Mexico in defiance of the derogatory imagery because watermelons also grew wild in Africa. So, eating watermelon among captured and enslaved Africans, especially those from the interior, was familiar—a connection to a homeland where they would never physically return. But food can transport and conjure memories of past lives and home. Realizing watermelons were part of African migration, Black Americans embraced the melon as a food connecting them to their homeland.

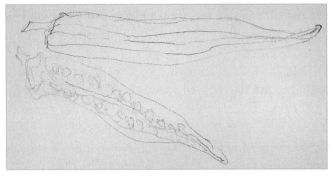

Okra. Illustration by author.

OKRA, CORN, AND TOMATO SUCCOTASH

Prep time: 20 minutes
Total time: 45 minutes
Serves: 6

Ingredients:
  1 lb. fresh okra, sliced in rounds
  2 tomatoes, peeled and sliced
  2 Tbsp. butter
  4 ears of corn kernels removed or 3 cups of whole corn kernels
  2 slices bacon
  1 medium onion, diced
  ⅓ cup canola oil
  1 celery stalk, diced
  1 red pepper, peeled and diced
  Creole seasoning, to taste

Preparation:
  In a large skillet, render the fat from two slices of bacon. Set bacon aside. Add ⅓ cup of canola to the pan. Cut okra into rounds and fry over medium heat until tender. Stir occasionally, turn the okra, and cook on both sides. Add red pepper to okra; continue cooking and stir. Add celery and onion to skillet and continue cooking, adding oil if necessary. Add corn to the skillet along with butter. Continue cooking for 4 minutes. Do not let it dry out; add butter. Adjust seasoning and serve.

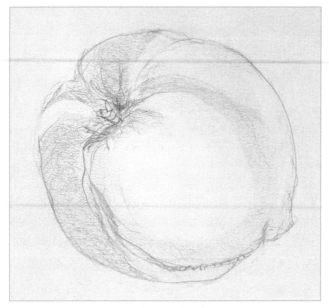

Peach. Illustration by author.

EASY PEACH COBBLER

Hands-on time: 20 minutes
Total time: 1 hour
Serves: 8–10

Ingredients:
  Topping:
  ½ cup sugar
  1 cup self-rising flour
  ¼ tsp. salt
  1 cup milk (oat milk)
  1 stick butter
  1–2 tsp. sugar
  ¼ tsp. freshly ground nutmeg
  cinnamon and brown sugar, to taste, optional

  Filling:
  1 28-oz can sliced peaches or 8 cups peeled, sliced fresh peaches
  ¾ cup granulated sugar

2 Tbsp. all-purpose flour
¼ tsp. salt
½ tsp. freshly grated nutmeg
4 Tbsp. butter, thinly sliced

Preparation:
Preheat oven to 350°F. Put 1/2 of the stick of butter in a pan (I use an iron skillet), but a 9- by 13-inch pan will work. Put in the oven to melt. Mix flour, sugar, and milk until well blended. Pour into pan. Combine peaches with every filling ingredient but butter. Dump peach mixture with juice evenly over the mixture without stirring. Cut the remaining butter and place it on top. Sprinkle cinnamon and brown sugar on top if using. Bake 30–40 minutes until golden brown. Top with vanilla ice cream.

Chapter Seven

FALL RETURNS AND GRANDPA DIES IN EARLY DECEMBER

FALL USHERED IN HOT AND WINDY DAYS THAT WERE HARD ON THE plants and the people, almost too hot for any crops to survive in dry farming, so Grandpa diverted whatever water he could from the lake. The rains still came, but they were warm and no match for the late summer heat. The cows suffered, too. Their massive lumbering bodies looked for cool places to rest. They gathered on a mound of rain-soaked soil, which was their best bet. Unfortunately, sometimes the ground was too dry, and when the rain finally came, another dry spell quickly followed, not allowing the earth to absorb much of the water.

But after everything was planted in the spring and harvested in the summer and early fall, Grandpa finally had time for himself and joined his Huntsman's Club members, a seasonal gathering of men for hunting trips in the late fall. As an accomplished huntsman, he served as a guide and camp cook for wealthy White hunter groups, guiding them through the waterways and woodlands to secure plenty of deer or ducks on their hunting trips. Neighbors knew when Grandpa went hunting. Well-known for his duck stew recipe, the aroma wafted out of the house through the screened windows and across the pastures, signaling to neighbors and friends that his hunting trip yielded many ducks, perhaps enough to share. Visitors suddenly showed up on the porch shortly after smelling the aromas.

"Papa got up early and went out with the White folk to shoot ducks and cook them up in a stew at the camp. He knew all the good hunting spots. He'd bring back so many ducks [that] he'd spread them out on the kitchen floor. We'd have duck for breakfast. My mother liked to cook, and she was a good cook. She fixed home-made biscuits every morning as part of our breakfast. It was common to have roast duck and biscuits for breakfast. She also made good cornbread from scratch, which we usually had with greens. My mother liked to cook, and she was a good cook."

—MOM

"He was a very good cook. When he went on hunting trips, he cooked a lot, duck stew and all kinds of stews."

—AUNT LILLY

Aunt Lilly also commented that her favorite recipe was the roast duck and dressing that their mother prepared after Grandpa's hunting trips. Grandpa's fall hunting trips were before the state sold its soul to the chemical and gas companies. But even then, you had to know where to hunt or fish to tread the murky water of the bayous safely. Grandpa knew how to look for the signs that the waters weren't suitable, and he taught his children to do the same. He dug a pond on his land to attract ducks to an isolated low area that thrived with silky grassy marsh plants that turned golden brown, mainly when the rains increased in the fall and winter months. The modest pond provided small fish, dryland vegetation, frogs, mallards, and wood ducks. Blue herons, white egrets, and sometimes even those big-bill pelicans scooped up a mouth full of fish before flying to larger bodies of water like Lake Pontchartrain. He allowed family and friends to fish in his pond, but it was off-limits to everyone else. Although the dairy was profitable, with so many mouths to feed, Grandpa always looked for other income sources.

"My father was so smart, [he] had wisdom. He built us a duck pond that had so many beautiful ducks with beautiful colors, green, purple, and orange."

—MOM

GRANDPA'S DEATH

In the late fall, my mother often spoke of her father's death as if she had memorized that day. She always started the same way: He started down the path to the barn, but this time through the front gate. Grandpa painted it with a fresh coat of paint every spring, according to the beliefs of Booker T. Washington and his cultivated approach to farm life. It was his last exit. Grandpa believed in taking pride and pleasure in his land—acting as a guardian of his plot of earth, planting trees for the generation to follow. Grandpa thought one's property, like oneself, should always be clean and presentable. It signaled his resistance to accept the life Whites planned for him. Instead, he created a home for his family built on his dairy farm outside the White gaze. He was born during Reconstruction, a hopeful time when people of color assumed roles in government to lead Louisiana into a more equitable future. But for those brave souls who tried governing, like C. C. Antoine and John Menard, the freedom to control during Reconstruction seemed like slavery with a different name.

Like Washington, Grandpa also came from a tradition of cultivating the land and an oral culture that transmitted a natural and sustainable way of planting, growing, and harvesting plants. Property ownership meant freedom. It was a type of activism and community uplift that enslavement denied. While Grandpa followed the progressive farming reform espoused by Washington, his only known father, John Bates, a North Carolinian, followed a more intuitive farming process that dates back to his enslavement days. Previously, the enslaved population created distinctly African American spaces that reinforced African and Black American cosmological traditions, their interpretation of the natural ordering of the universe in the wilderness, settled areas, and the crossroads.

But the morning when Grandpa transitioned, everything was normal. The giant willow tree was still inside the front yard fence. A few brown leaves still hung onto the thin weeping branches and flittered and sparkled as the early December wind pushed them back and forth from sunlight to shadows, and the gourd birdhouses crafted by their neighbor down the road swung in the breeze. The sagging gate still sagged. But for Grandpa, stepping off the porch onto the brick path was different this time. He approached the gate slower, with measured and halting steps.

Aunt Lizzetta said the last day of my grandpa's life was on a Saturday. On his way to town, he stopped to visit her before catching the streetcar. At the time, she was married to Clement Webb, one of her three husbands. "He was never happy over me marrying Clement in the first place," said Aunt Lizzetta. Grandpa took care of his business and rode the streetcar back to Allendale. When he arrived home on Talbot Street, he walked past the house and pasture to the barns instead of entering the house. His chest heaved to take in the precious air in this final season of his life. Yet, with this winter of his life coming to an end, he continued his debilitating walk to get into his life's work, his dairy.

"When he got to the big gate by the barn where you come into the little milk room and the barn, I think he died right there."

—AUNT LIZZETTA

He collapsed in the little milking room, organizing the milk for the market that had sustained his family for over three decades. He was gone; he had crossed over to the other side of the beautiful, beautiful river, having made that great transition in life in a split second.

In the distance, Grandma saw him as she exited the back door of the big, whitewashed house and ran past the chicken yard to the barn. Even before the steps of her narrow feet made it to his side, she knew that he was no longer of this world and that she had suddenly become head of the household and dairy. Her head, with upswept hair on top, spun at the thought of a future that came too fast. She felt alone as she considered what was before her, still amid an economic depression that had already claimed two hired hands on the dairy. The workers had depended on the dairy to feed and clothe their families, but Grandpa had to let some of them go, and being a man just turning sixty-six, he took on much of the work himself. Perhaps letting the men go and taking on extra work weighed heavy on his heart, knowing that grown men who had depended on him for so many years could no longer rely on him. What was the business he had in town? No one knew.

As Grandma found him in the milk barn, she wondered what would come of the family now. Life had been hard, but his family was among the privileged in their community—seemingly always having enough food, clothing, and even a little leftover. They would be fine. They would get along.

"Growing up in Shreveport, oh, the fun we used to have. We had everything we wanted. On Saturday, we could go to the movies, and the movie houses were segregated. So, the little old theater was called the Majestic Theater, but we'd have to sit up in the balcony. Honey, they've got a movie house on the avenue where our church was. I think it was twenty-five cents.

To ride the streetcar was a nickel though. And see, we would go to Sunday School; when we [would] leave for Sunday School, Mama would give us a nickel for carfare, a nickel to put in Sunday School, and a nickel to ride back home on, and a nickel to spend on an ice cream cone. So, we would walk to Sunday School and walk back home and spend the carfare on foolishness.

And it was a big store there. Papa left me at Castle grocery store, and we could go in there and charge things. On the way [home?] we'd walk by and if Castles grocery store was open, we could go in there and charge it to our father."

—AUNT LILLY

"Now we, the Bates family, were the only ones who had a phone. We would walk and call somebody on the telephone, which might be a block and a half, like if it was an emergency. But we had a telephone. Then Papa had a bathroom put on."

—UNCLE ANGUS

Memories of the man Grandma married in 1908 ran through her mind as her assortment of children, all two years apart, began pouring out of the house to discover their father in the milk room. He was a robust and big man with a commanding presence. He loved his children, and they loved him even though his stern stare kept them in order. But, on the other hand, their mother had a decidedly gentle touch—stopping to embrace them as they vied for a position under her thin arms. The sweet air of the morning began to melt away as they picked up Grandpa and brought him inside the house. The early morning glow had now seemed to turn a drab gray, and they laid him on a table in the parlor that Carrie Davis Bates had covered with a clean white sheet, fresh from flapping on the clothesline in the wind of yesterday's laundry. The only thing left was his burial.

After Grandpa's funeral, Grandma thanked her community for their thoughtful sympathies during the family's grief, but she had to continue as a partner in the dairy business. At the homegoing [to heaven], family members, neighbors, and friends celebrated Grandpa's life by bringing great bowls and plates of food to the house. Fried chicken and fish, baked ham, cooked greens, biscuits and syrup, cornbread, pound cakes, peach cobblers, and much more filled all the tables in the house. Grandpa's sons made vanilla ice cream, his favorite treat.

The chatter about their father grew louder, even now that he was gone. As folks suspected, Bates was not my grandpa's real name, as I later discovered. It was the last name of one of Grandma's sisters and her husband, John. When Grandpa's mother died during childbirth, they raised Grandpa as their son, but his mother named him Angus, perhaps after his birth father, a final act of defiance before leaving this world. My mother wasn't told much about her father, especially about adult secrets as a child. Then, many years following his passing, after she married and with her children, Aunt Lilly told Mom about their father.

> "Well, I don't know anything [about Papa's father], but they said he took the name from his aunt. His aunt's name was Bates. But they said his father was a White guy who came to San Francisco to live, and his name was Scott."
>
> —AUNT LILLY

I learned that Grandpa had lived in Shreveport for thirty-six years and owned the dairy for twenty-eight years. But Aunt Lilly's recollection of my grandfather's birth father stuck with me. She had gray eyes and straight hair like Grandpa and was the only sibling to settle in San Francisco. Did she know something that her other siblings did not know? Because, sometimes, she'd let little memories that she did not want to share with me slip into our conversations, signaling that Aunt Lilly knew more than she was willing to tell.

Inside the car: Aunt Alice, the driver, and Grandma are in the back seat.
Running rail: Cousin Clarence, Aunt Phoebe, Eloise, and Cousin Bobby.

"Papa and Mama worked as a team on the dairy. If Papa wasn't
working, he was at home except for going out with his hunting
club, but sometimes, he went off alone."
—ELOISE

When the children asked, "Where's Papa going?" Momma would
say he had some business to attend to, so Papa's business always meant
disappearing for my mother. The older brothers and sisters knew where
he was going, but the younger ones, like my mother, Booker T, Phoebe,
and Wilma, did not. Grandma made the older ones promise not to tell
the younger ones, so they didn't. My mother later found out he was
going to another farm nearby where the White folks stayed. Blacks
and Whites didn't mix, so why was he going over there? She heard her
brother Uncle Angus say that Papa's mother, my great-grandmother,
worked for the family who lived across the pasture toward Bossier City.

Papa knew the older man, and he visited him every month. He had two daughters and one son who left home. They said the son went out West before my grandpa's time.

> "Papa's mother was a brown-skin lady, and she got with a White man, and his two sisters could pass for Whites. The White man's family name that Dad's mom got with was Flournoy, and Papa changed his name to Angus Bates after when changing one's name from the given White name was legal. The Flournoy family was nearby, and Papa would talk periodically."
>
> —UNCLE ANGUS

Since Grandpa Angus was born and taken in by the Bates family, I guess it was only fitting that he took their name since they were the ones who raised him. But the problem was that the older Grandpa grew, the more he looked like, the older man's daughters across the pasture. He looked like the girls' brother, just a few shades darker. Tongues wagged, and gossip flew around that the son out West was probably his father. So, Grandpa Angus's visits down the road were possibly visits to his grandfather, but his children didn't want anything to do with my grandpa's family, and none of the older man's children wanted to have anything to do with them. Although there were tensions between the two families, for some reason, the older man wanted to see Grandpa every month, probably to look him in the face and to see his wayward son. Grandpa didn't find this out until he was a young man. Then, as he aged, he suspected something was wrong because he looked more like the children down the road, except for his color. Pointing fingers circulated in the town. "Did she give him some, or did he take it?" they said. Either way, a Black woman was always at the mercy of a White man, and a Black man couldn't do anything about it if he wanted to stay alive. It was just one of those painful situations that Black people had to steer around, not accepting but living with to exist in the Southern United States. In Louisiana, which had a long history of racial liaisons dating back to its French province, this was especially true. The trees that separated the dairy from the plantation pasture down the road were more than a property line. They were fault lines with a grandfather and his grandson living on opposite sides of the field.

"Papa visited the old man, and he came to the dairy to visit with
Papa, but Papa never spoke about the visits with his children."
—UNCLE ANGUS

Parents told their children about the barriers between Blacks and
Whites, especially the girls, about walking down roads alone, or about
known flashpoints where White men took young Black girls. Grandpa's
complexion and hair texture were a testament to the history of miscegenation in Louisiana. The children never understood what had happened
with him and his conception, but they knew that he was a product of
a liaison, and their skin color was also the product. It didn't matter
whether it was forced or consensual because it was terrible any way
you looked at it. The hushed silence surrounding his birth confirmed
a dreaded cultural taboo between Blacks and Whites. Jealousy from
his older siblings resulted in his childhood mistreatment. Although his
adoptive family shared the same skin tones, his mixed-race complexion
caused additional problems. His sisters could pass as White, but he
chose to live as Black. So, this genealogical discovery took me down
an unexpected path.

Mom was eleven when Grandpa died, and she remembers challenging times from her life on the dairy farm. Hearing stories about
the dairy, I still had questions about the family and Grandpa's father.
After years of combing through family history, I came up empty. Then,
I reflected on the house in Louisiana at my ninety-four-year-old Aunt
Lilly's home in San Francisco, cutting her hair and chatting about the
old days one afternoon. She had just given me a set of baby clothes from
Aunt Beaut that she had kept for a lifetime. She softly said, turning to
me as if pulling a long-held secret from her old memory:

"Papa had two mean sisters. One named Lena, and the other one,
I can't remember her name. They could pass for White. Honey,
Papa's papa was a White man named Scott, and he went to San
Francisco. His momma had some relatives named Bates."
—AUNT LILLY

Okay, so this was a known family secret. All I could think of was *Skillets in the Closet,* an assemblage by the artist David Hammons composed

of a narrow wooden closet, painted green and standing slightly open, exposing seven used and crusted cast-iron skillets hanging on hooks. Aunt Lilly knew that I was researching the family's history. Why hadn't she told me this before, especially when my questions hinted that I suspected something? My visits with her always included questions about our family's home in Louisiana. This was the first time she mentioned Grandpa's father. I turned to my mother, who also knew. Mom and all my aunts and uncles kept this secret from me. And then I thought about Aunt Lilly: is this why you chose to migrate to San Francisco rather than Los Angeles with the rest of the Bates family? Many years later, after her death, the family was going through her papers, and my sister found a bank receipt for a carpenter named Scott. Whether or not this has anything to do with the Scott she mentioned about my grandpa's family remains a question.

Grandpa had no brothers, at least by the same father and mother, and his sisters were by another father. His father could have lived just down the road in the "White section" of town, next to the adjoining pasture. Or his father could have been one of the newly arrived immigrants who first worked as vendors on the levee of the Red River that flowed up from New Orleans into this port in northwest Louisiana. Or he might have long gone to another part of Louisiana or out West, which is what a visit from a mystery man from San Francisco suggested. The liaisons were a part of the secrets of life, unspoken, something that Grandpa put in the recesses of his mind but something he couldn't ignore. So, because his birth father didn't entirely accept him, he often felt alone, and the trauma of living a lie weighed heavy on his heart. So, Grandpa decided to make the most of his life. As for the dairy, the sale deed said that he purchased it in 1907. But everyone in Allendale knew that the land between the edge of Cross Lake and Talbot Street and Holtzman and Hartman Streets was once a plantation belonging to the family on the other side of the fence. They knew because they and their families sharecropped that land; some were enslaved on the plantation before freedom came. Whatever the situation, sharecropping was a difficult existence. It also had profound social ramifications as cotton culture expanded into new regions of Louisiana in the decades after Reconstruction. By the early 1900s, the cotton kingdom had grown to include most of the upper Red River Valley, including Caddo, Bossier, DeSoto, and Claiborne parishes, along with most of northeastern Louisiana, central Acadiana, and parts of the Florida parishes. Few of these areas could be considered plantation areas, but the cotton regime took hold nonetheless, and with cotton came tenancy. Over 60 percent of cotton farmers were sharing tenants or sharecroppers rather than landowners.

As I wrote about my family's Lakeside Dairy, I always wondered about how they were able to live through such racially violent times for Black people. Louisiana's oppressive restrictions against Blacks made it difficult for them to have anything, let alone own something. Then, after viewing photographs of the Bates family that I had been looking at since I was a child, I considered something that had crossed my mind but that I chose to deny. But there it was as I rechecked the census records after completing the final edits for this book. My grandparents and their three oldest children, David, Janice, and Lilly, were classified as mulattoes. My grandfather Angus, who had worked for Miller Dairy, purchased his Lakeside Dairy in 1907 and was marked as mulatto under race in the 1910 census. I looked down at my grandmother Carrie's name, and she was listed as mulatto, as were their three young children. I then consulted the United States census history to understand this designation and how it changed for people of African descent through-out those early years of categorizing mixed-race people.

Of the fifty-one people listed living in their neighborhood of the fourth ward, only two owned businesses, an Italian grocer and the dairy-man, my grandfather. Most of his Black neighbors were either porters, laborers, or cooks. However, several Black women operated businesses in their homes as laundresses or seamstresses, as they were called in those days. I was surprised at the number of cooks working in private homes. Indeed, Black hands were stirring the pot, cooking, and season-ing foods, which signified the Black influence on Southern cuisine.[1]

Following the War of 1812, free people of color occupied a peculiar position in Louisiana, especially in New Orleans. There were distinct grades of society, and the Creoles, mulattoes as free people of color from other states, poured into Louisiana in a steady stream into his haven of refuge. It was an opportunity for enterprise and growth for people of color, especially the mixed race. But Whites feared the rising class of mixed-race people and further miscegenation.

John Willis Menard, the budding politician during Reconstruc-tion, was a writer born in Illinois, a free state, to parents who left New Orleans. He published *An Address to the Free Colored People of Illinois*.

In 1862, he became the first Black person hired as a clerk for the Department of Interior in Washington, DC, working under President Abraham Lincoln. Lincoln sent him to British Honduras to research that country as a possible colony for the "Negro problem." After separating from his first wife and child in Illinois, he moved to New Orleans after the Civil War. From there, he traveled to Jamaica and the US Virgin Islands, where he met Elizabeth Mary, married her, and had three children. Returning to New Orleans, he worked as a newspaper editor and ran for office on the Republican ticket for the second congressional district seat in Louisiana. He won but was challenged for office by the losing Democratic contender and was never seated. In 1868, free people of color had a larger share in their government than that class had in any other Southern state. Although Menard did not serve as a Congressman on February 27, 1869, in an eloquent appeal, he became the first Black person to address Congress. Although Louisiana thwarted his political ambitions, it did not deter them. He moved to Jacksonville, Florida, and in 1879, was appointed to the Florida House of Representatives and, in 1877, became the Duval County Justice of the Peace.[2]

But, as the legacy of Reconstruction continued, the initiation of Black Codes limited all Black people's freedoms, mixed race or not, and further separated the races and outlawed miscegenation. In Louisiana, as in many places, Reconstruction ushered in what felt like another form of enslavement. But, as Black people had done before, the more educated population continued to network with other Blacks in and outside their communities. In political organizations, churches, social clubs, and the opening of historically Black colleges and universities, they continued creating Black spaces for racial uplift. Menard's poetry in his 1879 collection of poems, *Lays in Summer Lands*, spoke to me, reminding me of the Black women who kept journals, and specifically my great-grandmother's *Life Sketches*.

In the 1920 census, my grandparents were still listed mulattos, but by the 1930s, mixed-race or lighter-skinned people were classified with a new term, "Negro," with a capital "N." The "one-drop rule," with variations, appeared in census instructions as early as the 1870s, so why did Louisiana census takers continue to use the terms "mulatto" and "mulatta" through the 1920s? This line of inquiry caused me to reassess the context of color privilege in my family by revisiting Louisiana's history. Most focus on the rise of free people of color, which began in the port city of New Orleans. And because Louisiana was a French colony and an important trading port, not only did goods come into the territory, but so did different types of people. Although described as immoral in terms of master and enslaved relationships, it was clear that the enslaved population continued to lighten in color as the city grew. Race-mixing was rampant, giving rise to a free Negro and Mulatto class. French and Spanish Creoles of lower Louisiana were always the advantaged class. These White-presenting Creoles considered the Creoles of color below them.

When I traveled to Shreveport in 2022, it wasn't easy to find anyone who knew my grandparents or their descendants since all of them had passed. My mother, the last surviving sibling, passed in San Jose, California, in 2020. My sister and I drove to the old dairy site, and the vacant single-story house had burned down. We drove around the neighborhood to find out what had happened to the house. A block away, the home of C. C. Antoine was torched and burned to the ground. Only the historical marker in front of the home remained. Then, we drove a block away past a church my grandfather helped build. No one knew any information about him or the family. Finally, we came upon a woman sitting on the porch of a house that looked like it would sink into the ground.

We introduced ourselves as the grandchildren of the man who owned the dairy down the street. She was bewildered. Then, an older gentleman came out of a door on the side of the house. We asked him about Grandpa and the dairy. He said, "Yeah, I heard of them. I didn't know them. You mean those light-skinned people, yeah, they lived there, they [people] told me about them," he said. I continued, "What do you know about them and the dairy?" He said, "I used to know about them, but since I had surgery on my tongue, it messed up my memory, and I can't remember much, but I remember hearing about the light-skinned people who lived there. They owned a dairy." I thanked him and moved on. We decided to go back to the church.

When I got to the church, a block from the old Bates home, I asked the ladies preparing for Sunday service if they knew of the Bates family. They didn't know the Bateses either, so they called the preacher on the phone. I spoke with him, but he was new to the area and didn't know much about them. "I think I heard about them and the dairy. Were they light-skinned?" he said. It appears that the Bateses' skin color was the one thing that stood out for both encounters. By all accounts, Grandpa was well-known in his community, but I'm sure many of his children were easily recognizable due to the light color of their skin.

"Everyone in the Allendale community knew the Bates family because there were so many of them."
—COUSIN SHONDA

Whatever happened, Grandpa was one of few who owned his dairy land, and like others of questionable birth, he made the best of his lot, rising above the circumstances and going on with his life. There were men like him, more well-known, like Booker T. Washington, whose father was also a White man, not willing to acknowledge his son publicly. However, hearing about Washington through Black news and organization networks gave Grandpa the strength to succeed. Since he had been brought up in a lie and knew a father didn't claim him, Washington became a father figure to follow like he was for many other rural Black men in the Southern farming communities. Although Washington had his critics, he inspired those in the Deep South who lived amid abject oppression and segregation. Washington's ability to forge a path of steppingstones to self-sufficiency that Black Southern men could follow helped them sustain lives for themselves and their families. It silenced Washington's critics, who had no experience of living in the hardships of the rural Southern landscape.

Grandma rebranded the dairy from LAKESIDE DAIRY to LAKESIDE DAIRY, C. D. Bates & Sons. Angus Bates's name had been on everything, and now it was her name. The children's father and mother always had other plans for them, and that time was coming, but Grandma wanted to sustain the dairy if she could stabilize the family. Her husband had worked hard to make way for his family, and she wanted to ensure that all the children could support themselves. So now, with clear eyes, she looked forward to the spring, committing to taking charge of Lakeside Dairy.

While Grandma held on, the legacy of the depression stretched, and it became clear to Grandma that changes were occurring in the dairy business. According to Uncle Angus, large dairies, like Metzger, purchased many small ones to create some of the largest dairies in northern Louisiana. Lakeside Dairy was the family's employer for many years, and with it gone, there were few options for work. It was either college or the military.

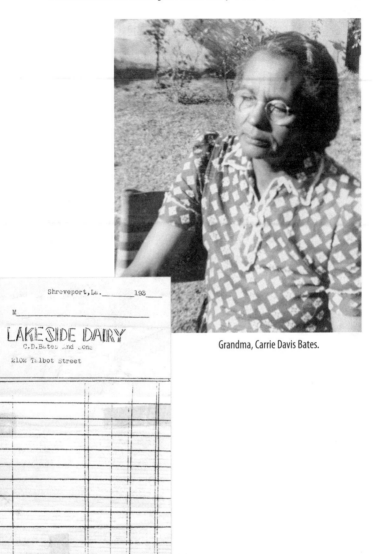

Grandma, Carrie Davis Bates.

Receipt from Lakeside Dairy, C. D. Bates & Sons, ca. 1935.

"After Papa died, Mama had a boyfriend named Mr. Blackwell. He lived across the hill. Mr. Blackwell would bring a delicious apple to Mama. Mama would cut the apple in half. Instead of eating the apple then she would take a teaspoon and dip it out at each side of the apple. Then she would give me the shell."

—MOM (ELOISE)

LOSING WILMA

"Wilma had red hair and freckles. They were giving shots at school, and when she got home, she told Momma that she didn't feel well. She came down with typhoid fever and died."
—MOM

Tall and lean like her mother, Wilma was one of the younger sisters in the Bates family. Born in 1922, she was two years older than my mother, Eloise. Wilma and Mom were close, perhaps the closest of the eight sisters, and when Mom spoke of Wilma to my sisters and me, she always referred to her as "Sweet Wilma." Mom, Wilma, and Aunt Phoebe, the youngest girl, shared the same bedroom in the two-story house. The three looked alike, especially Mom and Wilma, who had a quiet way about her, harboring many thoughts to herself. She didn't even share them with her brothers and sisters. But she was a smart "go-getter," Mom said, inspiring her younger sisters to study and learn what her brothers were learning.

"Wilma was a son of a gun. Mama told Wilma it's your time to wash the dishes. And Wilma said, I wish I was a chicken [so I wouldn't have to wash dishes]! Ooh, Mama said if you were a chicken, you'd have to eat poo-poo and everything else!"
—AUNT LILLY

"They wouldn't let us get away with leaving dirty dishes. Lula and me went to bed one night and didn't wash the dishes. Papa would get up at three o'clock in the morning. He got us up at three o'clock to wash those dishes."
—AUNT LIZZETTA

The four boys learned different aspects of the dairy business and the management of the animals. They also traveled to town to pick up the feed, milk the cows, and help their father run the dairy because when their father could no longer manage the day-to-day business, they would fill his shoes. Likewise, the eight girls learned domestic skills on the dairy farm, like ironing, sewing, quilting, cooking, canning foods in glass jars, and processing the dairy milk into other products like butter, yogurt, and cream.

But they also tended the kitchen garden with their mother and picked fruits and nuts from their trees. Most of all, the older girls, like Aunt Mabel, who won honors in the class of 1932 at Central Colored High, counted the money earned from selling the dairy's milk products. They accounted for every cent earned, saved, and spent with their mother. A younger daughter, Wilma was incredibly ambitious at keeping the records. But, aside from celebrating her business acumen, no one said much about Wilma except that she was a freckled-faced redhead girl. I think of her often because her red hair gene leaped over a generation to my eldest son, the only other Bates descendant with reddish hair, which has now darkened. However, his son's hair is reddish too. Family genes hop, skip, and jump.

Wilma loved juicy, deep purple blackberries. She'd often pick and eat them, veering off the path from school to the edge of Louisiana's low-lying areas filled with backwater from heavy rains that took too long to drain. Wilma thought that parts of the water looked funny and still. It smelled terrible, too, so she went further up to rinse her blackberries in the water that rippled over the rocks of the stream. Wilma knew better than to drink the water, but, against her better judgment, using a little water to clean her berries seemed ok. She often challenged the conventional wisdom of her elders and went her own way. She didn't realize that the contaminated water could compromise her immune system.

It was time to immunize school-age children in Allendale schools. Parents, including my grandmother, agreed that immunization was the best course of action to keep the community free of dreaded diseases like typhoid fever, measles, and polio. She surmised that if the president of the United States could get polio, her children could too. Although the children shuddered at the thought of a needle going into their arms, their parents trusted the health officials. Immunization day came, and the clean and sparkling children stood in a line waiting their turn. Wilma didn't feel well. She had started her period the day before and had painful cramps. She went to school anyway because she wanted her injection and strived for perfect attendance that year.

When school let out, she didn't veer off the path to her home to pick her favorite blackberries. She came straight home. Wilma didn't feel well at home, and she told her mother. The health officials warned the parents that the injections could sometimes make people sick like they had the flu. They considered it a small price to pay to protect the children's health in the community. Because Wilma was menstruating, Grandma told her to go upstairs and nap. She couldn't sleep and tried to rest, but her severe headaches increased. Grandma went upstairs, got cold water from the indoor bathroom faucet, and filled a white, blue-rimmed graniteware washing bowl. She entered the room Wilma shared with her sisters with a clean, wet facecloth and laid it across Wilma's head. Grandma thought the headache, like others that girls experienced during their month, would pass, but Wilma's body was so hot. Her condition worsened. Her lunch came up, and she was weak. Grandma called Dr. Powell, the family doctor, and when he arrived, he found Wilma listless and wringing, wet with a high temperature, with small hives forming on her skin. He gently placed his fingers on her wrist and took her pulse. He could barely feel it beat. Trying to understand the illness, the doctor asked Grandma if Wilma had been anywhere recently or eaten anything unusual. Grandma showed the doctor the blackberry stains on Wilma's fingers. He asked Wilma, "Where did you pick them?" "At the backwater near the sawmill," she replied timidly because that was off-limits for the Bates children. It was a wild place where too many bad things happened. People mysteriously disappeared over there. Plus, if the berries there were not ripe, they could make you sick. Grandma said the only other place she had been in the past few days was to school, and "today she got a shot with the other children." She also mentioned that Wilma was on her period.

Looking at Wilma, the doctor asked if the person giving her the shot knew she was on her cycle. With a downturned head, Wilma shook her head back and forth, signaling no, being too shy to reveal something that personal. Dr. Powell immediately thought of an infection born of a perfect storm of circumstances. He surmised that Wilma might have eaten something contaminated, perhaps the blackberries, which weakened her system. Being on her period also affected her immune system, and she received an injection to stave off typhoid fever. Although he diagnosed an infection, he was unsure of the type, but he had an idea. He knew that whatever compromised her immune system, he had to act quickly. He took a blood sample and told her to drink plenty of liquids until he returned later that night. Once he returned to his office, he tested her blood, confirming his suspicions: Wilma had typhoid fever.

Now that he knew for sure, he had to treat her immediately. Luckily, his office was in Allendale's Texas Avenue business section, near the dairy. As a Black doctor, he couldn't have an office downtown with the other White doctors. Returning to the Bates home, Grandma asked the doctor if Wilma got the virus from ingesting bad food or water. As it turns out, the contaminated blackberries set things in motion—weakening her system. He later discovered that with so many students receiving immunizations that day, healthcare workers were speeding the children through the line, perhaps reusing needles, puncturing some children's arms with the same syringe. The unsanitary mishap infected Wilma's blood, and already losing blood from her period, her body couldn't fight the infection. After realizing what compromised her immune system, the doctor treated her with a vaccine, but it came too late for Wilma. A few days later, she died at age seventeen of typhoid malaria.

Her mother was at her wit's end because she had faith in the health workers who came to the school. She thought they would take all precautions to ensure her children's health. So how was Grandma to know that one of her young daughters, the freckled-faced flaming redhead Wilma, would die in her teens—fading away after receiving an injection at school that was supposed to save her life from a disease? It was a careless and preventable mistake. Wilma was one of those sad tragedies in immunization history in the US. After her burial, my grieving grandma thanked her community for the kindness they had shown the family in their time of loss.

"We cannot thank you all personally, [so] we take this way of telling you how much we appreciate your sympathy and kind assistance extended to us at the time of our late bereavement. Especially we do thank our friends, churches, and schools for the florals and other remembrances. Only those who have been shown similar kindness when they most needed it can understand our feeling toward all of you."
—MRS. CARRIE BATES AND FAMILY

It was many years before Grandma came to terms with Wilma's passing. It wasn't like losing a child at birth. She had watched Wilma grow into a young woman, surviving the period's other deadly childhood diseases. Grandma envisioned a bright future for her daughter. She looked forward to her knocking down social, political, and racial walls. Yes, Wilma was going to be the daughter who did that. After her death, a doctor came to the house to check all the children for typhoid. None of them had the disease, only Wilma, because it was possibly injected directly into her bloodstream. The children only spoke of Wilma in the context of her death and the events leading to that tragedy. It was apparent that whenever they went to that space in their heads and hearts where they kept her in their memory, they were still in disbelief that it had ever happened.

When Grandpa died, some of his children had already entered college. At the time, two of my aunts, Beaut and Lilly, attended Wiley College, one of the oldest historically Black colleges west of the Mississippi. It was close to their Allendale home, near the Texas border in Marshall.

Aunt Lilly with an axe at the woodpile.

Cousin Doris, Grandma, and Cousin Ronald.

Wiley College was founded by the Freedman's Aid Society of the Methodist Episcopal Church in 1873, turbulent times for Blacks in America. Wiley opened south of Marshall, Texas, with two buildings.

Aunt Lilly graduated from college, returned home, and married, and she and her new husband moved into one of the second-floor bedrooms. Like many other college-educated women, Aunt Lilly took a teaching job at a country school until she could save money to purchase her home. Homeownership was a sign of financial success. The household dynamics at my grandmother's home also changed without Grandpa. She still had three high-school-age children and now another male residing there, who was not part of the original Bates family. Cousins, Uncle David's children, whose mother died, had known the Bates siblings since childhood. They had grown up with them and were always welcomed.

While Uncle Angus was away at school, Booker T and Uncle David, who had been in the army, once discharged, returned to the dairy to help with the day-to-day operations. But Cousin Anita said Uncle David, nicknamed Bubba, wasn't too good at the job.

"David loved women, and before he remarried, he always took eggs from the farm, milk, butter, and cream cheese and gave them to his women friends. However, he was not much of a businessman and didn't like the hard manual labor needed to run a dairy, especially since the hired hands were let go."

—COUSIN ANITA

Young Uncle David with a cow, standing in front of the lake.

Uncle David must have learned something working on the dairy because he later moved to Waskom, Texas, and opened his dairy. He remarried and started his second family. The only brother that remained
was Uncle Booker, who was working, waiting tables at a hotel, and a
new grown man entered the household. This changed the dynamics of
the house as the girls, like my mother, one of the youngest of Grandma's
daughters, would soon find out.

The parlor, a room of society and goodwill meetings, sometimes
had its dark side. As family members aged and talked about their lives
working on the dairy and living in their father's two-story home, they
revealed a few negative happenings in that home. There were so many
children, but it was a big house. According to my mother, Eloise, one
of the younger school-aged children remaining at home, she felt uncomfortable with her sister's husband in the house.

"I liked to go into the parlor to take a nap. It was quiet. I'd be alone sleeping, but then I'd feel someone [looking at me]. I'd crack my eyes to see a figure standing at the doorway, breathing hard. It was Roy. I pretended that I was asleep. I never told anyone then. But I always thought he was sneaky."

—MOM

Aunt Lilly must have suspected something because she always protected her little sister, Eloise, even after she married and had my sisters and me. Aunt Lilly had these protective feelings for my mother until she died at one hundred years old. After that, my mother shared her feelings about her sister and husband. We wondered if Aunt Lilly watched over Mom because she mistrusted her husband around her younger sister.

THE MULE AND THE PLOW

The older children left home to find jobs to support the dairy and the family. Mabel went to Philadelphia, the stepchildren Lena and Leonard went to Los Angeles, and David joined the army. Aunt Beaut had graduated from Wiley, when Lilly was in her second year of college before Grandpa died. Angus got accepted into college at Southern University in Baton Rouge but took a break from Southern to help with the dairy. Lilly returned to Wiley and completed her degree while Angus helped his brother Booker T. Once Lilly graduated, Angus returned to college.

"When they went away to Wiley College, one time, I remember asking her [Grandma] how much money we had, and she said, '$25,000 in the bank from the dairy.' Only professionals went to college at that time. They turned out to be teachers. My Dad passed my first year at Southern. I went back the second year but then stayed out [to help on the dairy]. When I returned, my mom said there's no money here in Shreveport."

—UNCLE ANGUS

Since his mother said there was no money in Shreveport, Uncle Angus left college and began caddying at the Shreveport Country Club. His initiative in doing other work like washing glasses for the tournament impressed his head chef. He asked him to return to work that following Monday. He ended up carving out a steady job with the Country Club. His younger siblings also took jobs to generate income for the family.

> "Soon after, the chef told me, 'Mr. Bates, why don't you become a waiter?' I would load up the plates for the banquets. I was seventeen years old and the youngest one there, so they relied heavily on me because the other banquet waitpersons were older and couldn't lift as much weight. I started waiting tables. I used to stack quarters, silver, and half dollars and put them on my mother's dresser. 'It's three stacks of money there.' I said, 'Mom—take that money.' She said, 'I don't want that money because it's dishonest, and you're stealing.' She didn't believe I was making that much money."
>
> —UNCLE ANGUS

> "Booker T also waited tables at the Washington Youree Hotel, making seventeen to eighteen dollars a night. It took Booker T coming back home to convince my mother that it was honest money that I'd make in tips and salary."
>
> —UNCLE ANGUS

> "As a teenager, I got a job at Pig Markham making sausages during the summer. I also had a job for a while folding papers for the *Shreveport Times* newspaper."
>
> —ELOISE

Working for the hotel convinced Uncle Angus that he needed to return to school. So, after working in the hotel for a few months, he earned $450 by the beginning of school. He told the dining hall lady he needed a job or couldn't stay in school. She said they needed help, and she wanted to hire him, but the school didn't have the funds to hire more services. But good fortune visited him. When he almost ran out of money, a job came up washing pots and pans. He took the job, which lasted the rest of his time in college. After that, he did not have to pay tuition again. In that regard, Southern was very good to him. He knew that working, unlike his sisters, was the only way he could pay for his education.

"After graduation, three days later, my buddies and I were still hanging around, eating three meals a day, using the facilities, etc. The Dean of Men knocked on our door. He said, 'Men, this school has done all it can for you. It is time for you to leave.' It was heartbreaking. I got a job at a hotel and made nineteen dollars a night."

—UNCLE ANGUS

Black colleges were part of an informal economy, especially for Uncle Angus. He took classes in his major coursework and worked in the cafeteria to defray his tuition. In the process, he became familiar with the workings and tools of the kitchen and the preparation of meals for large numbers of students. The campus was his new community, his community of people with common goals of education. The schools were Black spaces of higher learning, away from the oppressive challenges of Jim Crow. They were also a place where they could freely address the issues of upward mobility and navigate how to overturn Jim Crow. His Dean of Men telling him and his classmates they had to leave meant he had to reenter a world of limited possibilities. However, the Black college experience taught the students what Black freedom looked like.

After working at the hotel briefly, Uncle Angus went to Los Angeles to visit his siblings. When he returned home with his degree in agriculture and chemistry, he wanted to gain teaching experience like Aunt Lilly before returning to Los Angeles. Uncle Angus began teaching at a rural Shreveport school four months after graduating while helping his family with the dairy part-time. The White school superintendent asked him to demonstrate to his Black students how to plow fields with a mule, forbidding him to teach them what he had learned in college. For Uncle Angus, it was too much like tenant farming. With a major in chemistry and a mastery of progressive farming techniques, he planned to introduce advanced farming techniques taught at HBCUs. He had always worked on the dairy with his father, who was forward-thinking, encouraging the younger Angus to go to college and learn more. In frustration, he left his teaching post.

"Angus stopped plowing, tied the mule to a tree, and left his job. Angus came home and told Mama [Grandma] he had given up his job. Mama pleaded for Angus to go back and take the forty-dollars-per-month job. That's when Angus left for Los Angeles."

—COUSIN ANITA

Uncle Angus knew he could do better. Thousands of Black Louisianans had already begun migrating out of Louisiana in the early twentieth century for better jobs in industrial complexes, educational opportunities, and to escape the yoke of Jim Crow society with its beatings and lynching. Rural areas with small towns like Allendale, surrounded by cotton fields, experienced the devastation of the infestation of the boll weevil. While the dairy was still afloat, unemployment from agricultural jobs, like cotton, left many workers without work. Some turned to work in the timber companies. Grandma didn't want Lakeside Dairy to close, so Uncle Angus stayed to help his younger brother Booker T and his mother with the dairy.

However, historical events related to World War II greatly enhanced the overall opportunities for Black people. Unfortunately, it also created a death knell for the dairy regarding worker retention. In June 1941, President Roosevelt responded to complaints about discrimination against Black Americans in all war-related work in the defense industry. He issued Executive Order 8802 on June 25, 1941, directing that Black Americans be accepted into job-training programs in defense plants, forbidding discrimination by defense contractors, and establishing a Fair Employment Practices Commission (FEPC). President Truman dismantled the FEPC, but in December 1946, he appointed a panel named the President's Commission on Civil Rights to promote anti-lynching and anti-poll tax laws, strengthening protections for Blacks. On July 26, 1948, his Executive Order abolished segregation in the armed forces, ordering full integration of all branches. Some Southern congressmen and factions in the military resisted full integration, but the Korean conflict strengthened the need for Blacks in the military. By the end of that conflict, segregation, at least on paper, ceased. But the oppression and hardships that threatened their very existence continued as White violence rose against Blacks through the 1930s. The second Great Migration West continued as Blacks packed up and left the oppressive conditions under which they lived in the South for better job and educational opportunities.

When Grandma decided to close the dairy and began selling off pastureland, most of her children had already left Louisiana to take advantage of federal job opportunities or enter the armed service. Much of the Black migration experience centered on creating a better life for their children and opportunities for full citizenship, which meant the right to vote. The disenfranchisement of Black people continued into the 1960s and 1970s. By then, I had freely voted in local and national elections. Leaving home for the Bates siblings meant they could build and sustain their lives with dignity and support their mother back home. One by one, each sibling set out to build lives independent of the dairy, and it was clear that the dairy could not exist without the care and labor of family members.

Many Blacks from Louisiana and Texas migrated to California, where I was born. Grandmother ran the dairy until 1943, closing it during World War II. Roosevelt's executive order weakened incentives to remain on family farms and thus was a blow to Black farming. With fewer laborers available and her children leaving the South for better opportunities, a family-owned dairy was untenable. There was no one to milk the cows and drive the milk to market, no cream for coffee, no butter to churn, cream cheese to sit on the hearth to firm, and no yogurt to ferment. Grandma continued to rent out the pasture for cattle to graze but had to sell her small herd and pigs because no one was home to tend to the animals. She had laid off the last field hands, so the land became fallow. There was nothing to sell but fruit from the trees that encircled the home site, vegetables from her garden, and eggs from the chickens who roamed the yard. She still tended her flowers and gave them away to anyone wishing to collect a bunch.

Continuing education beyond high school invariably meant leaving home and the dairy for work opportunities. In their community, teaching was a noble profession that educated the masses of the underserved community that remained in the chokehold of segregation. But the pay was low and supplies inadequate. Even then, the young adults who could pursue teaching were lured away by the stories about finding better-skilled jobs outside the South. Although wishing for her family to be near her, Grandmother understood the reality and dynamics of growth and opportunity. She had prepared her children for this next phase in their lives, even if it meant leaving her. With the beginning of World War II, Louisiana created new jobs, but Jim Crow's social oppression was choking their progress. California was a better choice for advertised defense industry jobs.

"I went for an interview at the Los Angeles Athletic Club and was hired as a waiter. This White captain approached me on my last day and told me I was a good waiter. It was a no-tips job, but after a while, I was told I was good and started making tips. Soon after,

I started working in the banquet room and started making more money. I learned how to cook from waiting tables, and when I got married, I had to learn to do it from necessity. My wife never cooked. I'd feed Angela, my daughter. Mom did all the cooking on the dairy. None of the other kids shadowed her in the kitchen, but I learned to cook in hotels and restaurants."

—UNCLE ANGUS

Although Uncle Angus didn't cook at home, his family lived off the land, growing and raising foods that made their way onto the family's table and into the homes of the community that the dairy serviced. But he had worked from the field to table all his life, and now, in urban Los Angeles, he wanted more.

DUCK GUMBO

Uncle Angus was known in my mother's family for his gumbo because of his yearly fishing trips to southern Louisiana. An avid angler, he specialized in seafood gumbo. My husband, Willie, also made a "stomp down" gumbo. Okra or nkombo, as it is known in West Africa, is at the core of a good bowl of gumbo in our family, a signature meal for Christmas dinner that must come with an ample amount of king crab legs. Saying both words one after the other, it is understandable how nkombo became gumbo among enslaved Louisiana populations.[3]

Everyone talked about the number of ducks Grandpa brought home from his hunting trips and the aromatic smells from his stew. My family decided to have duck on our Christmas menu in memory of Grandpa, and instead of stew, we created a duck gumbo, preparing the roux with duck broth. I didn't include a version of Grandpa Angus's duck recipe in this book. Unfortunately, I couldn't find the recipe written down anywhere, and I could only go on my aunts' and uncles' descriptions. This duck gumbo homage to Grandpa is rich in taste and memory. We were all surprised at our gumbo, feeling that he had a hand stirring our pot.

Hands-on time: 1 hour
Total time: 2 hours
Serves: 6 to 8

Ingredients:
1 duck, approximately 4–5 lb.
1 cup canola oil
1 cup all-purpose flour
1 green bell pepper, cored and diced
3 cups yellow onions, diced
5 large garlic cloves, chopped
2 cups diced celery
1 lb. smoked or Andouille sausage, cut into rounds
2 quarts duck stock, made from cooking cut-up duck
1 cup diced parsley
2 tsp. gumbo filé (a seasoning powder)
3 bay leaves
2 tsp. kosher salt
2 tsp. black pepper
¼ cup Creole seasoning
2 tsp. dried thyme

Preparation:

THE STEW

Brown and simmer ducks on medium fire with 1 cup onions, 1 cup celery, 2 cloves garlic, and parsley in a Dutch oven until well-browned; remove and set aside. Make a roux (see below). While the roux is cooking, add the sliced fresh okra in rounds in a separate skillet and sauté over medium heat with ¼ cup of oil until tender (approximately 7 minutes; add additional oil if necessary). Heat ¼ cup of oil in the Dutch oven. Add remaining celery, onion, garlic, and bell pepper and cook until tender, then add the sausage and cook until done. Add the cooked roux to the onion, celery, bay leaves, bell pepper, sausage, and thyme and stir well. Next, mix the cut-up duck and sautéed vegetables well and pour in the duck stock. Let this slowly simmer for approximately 45 minutes. Add seasoning of salt and pepper to taste. Serve over rice, and add parsley as a garnish.

THE ROUX

To make the roux, pour the oil into the Dutch oven to cook the duck and let it heat up over low. Then slowly add the flour, sprinkle it to cover the oil, and whisk until well combined. Let the flour cook for approximately 20 minutes until the color changes to a dark brown, stirring with a whisk every 2 to 3 minutes, making sure it does not burn. If it burns, start over. Set aside when cooked.

Chapter Eight

THE LEGACY AND HISTORICAL AND CULTURAL CONTEXT OF LAKESIDE DAIRY

CAPTIVATED BY STORIES ABOUT COUNTRY LIFE ON THE DAIRY FARM, A teaching position for my husband at Tuskegee University offered me an opportunity to experience the rural South. Since the job was temporary, I first expected to remain in Santa Barbara with the children and continue my teaching position there. That changed when Tuskegee offered me a job, too.

My husband was born in a small community in northern Louisiana and was happy to return to semirural life. Born in Los Angeles and a Californian all my life, I resisted the relocation. I finally agreed to leave the West Coast to embark on a Southern adventure. My mother was born in Louisiana, and my father was born in East Texas. I wanted to learn more about the region that connected so many Black people in the Los Angeles neighborhood of my youth.

The university had a sizeable, stately dairy barn—much larger than I could ever imagine my grandfather having. But, seeing it as I leaned on a fence, staring at it, resting silently in the tan fall landscape, all cows gone, still, made me think of Grandpa. Even as my two young boys climbed unsteadily on the railings of the fence and my husband rested on the stroller with a third son tucked in, silently sleeping, I was there alone with my grandfather's legacy. It was then that I began wanting to know more about him. I queried family members, which started my journey back through the stories I had heard all my life. I took them for granted then, but now I do not.

In the South, we lived at wood's edge. A piney smell from the wood-lands permeated our home as the pathless woods were a few paces away. A dense wall of pine trees seemed foreboding, a place where one, especially young children, could easily get lost. "Do not go into the woods," I cautioned my small ones as they played outside because the land elevation dropped quickly, reminding my husband of the "old place" behind his family home. A freshwater creek ran below in a densely wooded ravine. He recounted the folk tale about "coachwhip" snakes that lived in such areas. He recited the story as we headed for the "old place" with his father's horse, Charlie, on a visit to his family farm in Columbia, Louisiana, an inactive northcentral riverboat town near the Ouachita River.

THE COACHWHIP SNAKE INCIDENT

Daddy always went down to the old place and into the holler in the northcentral Louisiana countryside. It was the land his father settled in after slavery. First, he had to walk down a hill into the woods full of pine, sweetgum, and oak trees. Plenty of blooming magnolia and dogwood trees peeked out between the pines. Then, he carefully led his horse Charlie by his bridle over the vines and branches that had fallen from the trees to a plentiful forest with dried wood to chop. After he cut the wood, he bundled it up tightly with a rope and tied it to Charlie's saddle so he could haul it back to the house. Charlie had to watch his steps because he could trip. Daddy was always careful, too, because the holler was known to have snakes slithering around on the ground. Sometimes, they hung from the trees.

One day, Daddy went to the holler for some wood. Like he always did, he took Charlie with him. But this time, he decided to ride on Charlie's back instead of leading him into the holler with his bridle. Once Daddy chopped the wood, he split a few pieces to make a slide to haul the bundle of tied timber up the hill. Then, he used a long rope to fasten the bundled wood to Charlie's saddle. Finished with his task, he looked forward to getting home for supper. However, Daddy was tired, and instead of walking Charlie, he hopped onto the saddle and rode up the hill for home. Charlie tried to tow the tight bundle of wood, but the extra weight with Daddy made his load too heavy.

Suddenly, something slithered out of the bushes onto the ground in front of Charlie's feet. It frightened Charlie, and he lost his footing with the heavy wood and Daddy on his back. He bucked, throwing his black head backward and Daddy out of the saddle. Then Daddy heard something like a whip crack. Charlie started to jump around. Daddy saw a long pink coachwhip snake stretching over three feet and with a green head. He picked up a thick log and threw it at the snake, but he missed. The coachwhip cracked his whip at him. Charlie started running up the hill with the bundle of wood in tow. Daddy chased Charlie, and the snake chased Daddy, cracking his whip the whole while. Daddy grew more tired and had to stop running. He didn't see the snake. He remembered that snakes are cold-blooded animals and move fast, but they could soon tire of chasing after you. He also heard that if it catches you, it will wrap its body around your legs and whip you with its tail. Daddy did not want that.

Daddy rested too long. Then he turned around and saw the snake staring directly into his eyes. Building up his courage, Daddy said to the coachwhip snake, "Get thee behind me." It was something that the preacher at his church said to the devil. The snake stopped and coiled up to strike, but Daddy pulled a heavy stone from behind his back that he picked up while running away. Staring the coachwhip snake straight into the eyes again, Daddy repeated, "Get thee behind me," and threw the stone and hit the snake on the head. It wasn't dead, but it couldn't see Daddy leapt and ran up the hill and out of sight. He ran as fast as his feet could carry him, hopping over fallen tree branches, through bramble bushes, between the vines, and into a clearing where he saw his house. He almost flew over the white picket fence into the yard.

Charlie stood there, breathing hard, waiting for him, with the cut wood still tied to his saddle. Both Charlie and Daddy made it home safely with the wood. When his father asked Daddy what happened, he said, "I collected the wood, tied it into a bundle, made a slide to tow the wood, tied it to the saddle with a rope, and I got on Charlie's back to head home, and a snake attacked us." His father said, "You mean you got on Charlie's back with a load of wood tied to the saddle?" "Yes," Daddy said, bowing his head. "That was your mistake. You were supposed to pull Charlie up the hill and watch the ground around him for snakes. Snakes sneak up behind you when they think you aren't watchin'. You'll know better the next time I send you to get wood in the holler," his father scolded him. His son lowered his head at the thought of returning down in the holler to the home of the coachwhip snake. "But," his father said laughingly, "I'm glad you hit that snake in the head and brought home the wood."

Oddly enough, during the fall months in Tuskegee, I took my children on excursions each morning on a woodland path—a shortcut, not more than an opening where I had to bend down to fit through a tunnel of blackberry branches. The weather was calm now, and snakes were hibernating. On this path to their school, they'd find tadpoles and salamanders, but we'd let them be. I am deathly afraid of spiders, and now I can't even imagine navigating my two oldest boys through the woods. At the time, they were about four and six years old. When other neighborhood kids learned about our walk, they asked their mothers if they could go to school with us. Two other children joined our little group for a short walk through the woods. It was a parade of children playfully galloping down the street of neatly cared-for brick homes with manicured lawns that ran up to a wild hedge. Before entering, a third child joined us. We turned a corner behind flowering azalea hedges. Lowering our bodies, we suddenly vanished into the wilderness. It may be surprising that parents let me take their children on this little adventure before school. At the end of our short trek, the children saw St. Joseph's Catholic School across the play yard. I waved goodbye to them, ensuring they joined the other children before turning around and heading back through our tunnel through the wooded path.

Still, we were in the land and legacy of the celebrated plant scientist George Washington Carver, who was known to walk the fields and woodlands of the university in the early morning sun. In his cracking brown leather lace-up shoes, he picked a fresh flower for the lapel of his sagging jacket. This gentle and soft-spoken soul known for his experiments with peanut byproducts found solace and solitude in his chemistry laboratory and in an atmosphere where the paintings he created didn't receive the same respect as his scientific experiments. Yet, he continued to marry science with his creative expressions, especially his paintings. At the university, I learned that Carver excelled at making crafts, including crocheting intricate doilies, weaving baskets from long needle pines, drawing botanical illustrations of plants for his published Bulletins, and pursuing the art of painting flowers he grew. His favorite flower was the amaryllis, a red one he discovered through experimentation in his laboratory. I did not know this flower when I came to Tuskegee to teach art appreciation and art history. But as I walked down my street visiting with neighbors, who all worked in some capacity for the university, I noticed red amaryllis flowers in their flowerbeds. When I asked about the flowers, they all referred to Dr. Carver. In some way, their flower bulbs came from him and populated private residences surrounding the university in Macon County.

As our family settled into life in Tuskegee, I could see that my husband was happy to be in a place that looked and felt like his home in Louisiana, and he quickly embraced farm life once again. But then he said, "Let's buy a pig for the winter. That way, we'll know where our pork comes from." "Excuse me?" I chimed. A stomp-down farm boy, he was into fresh produce, meats, and poultry, and he had an intimate relationship with the reality of eating from the whole hog. Like my grandparents, his family ate from their field, slaughtered their animals for beef, and smoked pork, which became hams, bacon, and sausages they shared with extended family members and neighbors who were just a holler away. So, I begrudgingly complied and went about locating a pig. A former farm extension agent recommended Mr. Sistrunk, a local farmer.

Once we arrived at his farmhouse, he offered to drive the children to the pigpen in the back of his mule-driven wagon as we followed in our car. They climbed into the back of Mr. Sistrunk's wooden wagon with their bodies rattling as he steered it down the dusty road to find their pig. Our excited children jumped out of the wagon when we reached the pigpen and ran over to the pigs. There were four little piglets. They chose a spotted one and called it Spotty. I felt kind of unsure about giving their pig a name. I didn't know if they realized their pig would season our beans or be on our breakfast table as bacon and sausage during the winter and spring. The children fed their pig on our visits to the Sistrunk farm, but as the pig grew, we lessened our visits. By slaughtering time, we replaced the pig with a black Labrador retriever puppy that they named Todo, which occupied all their free time. My husband and I went to pick up Spotty's remains. We didn't take the whole hog—we left Mr. Sistrunk the feet, snout, ears, tail, intestines, all parts of the pig that country people refused to throw away. I wasn't going that far in my house. It was enough to have the pig meat. We divided the pig into manageable parts so that each section still had the skin to save for cracklings. Many Black people with Southern roots have barbecue stories. My father, who we called Pop, was a Texan. He loved barbecue, but it was too greasy for mom. I could take it or leave it, but my husband came from a farm family that smoked meats and grilled them on open fires. He preferred wood fires to charcoal grills because they gave meats, poultry, fish, and vegetables the flavor and aroma of the wood.

While in the South, we also had venison—deer is a staple during the winter months, along with ducks and freshly caught fish. Church members brought us so much squash and collard, turnip, and mustard greens that I didn't have to plant any. Instead, my husband took up winemaking, using scuppernongs, a "grape" native to the Southern US. His enology club members included many of the university's chemists, biologists, botanists, and horticulturalists. One year, they won the silver medal in a southeast winemaking competition in Atlanta.

In Tuskegee, as ice glistened on the pine needles, the cold wind sucked up the air, and the wet winter took hold. We huddled around the fireplace, especially when the towering pine trees snapped during the ice storms. There was little work outside for the farmers like Mr. Sistrunk during these times. So, my outside visits to the sunny porches turned inward to sitting in front of the cozy fireplace with old farmer Sistrunk, cracking pecans from the trees encircling his house. Then, we'd step through the front door of his home, where he greeted us almost in a whisper, "How yawl doin'?"

DRIVING FROM TUSKEGEE TO FISK UNIVERSITY IN A BLACK RAG-TOP RED VOLKSWAGEN CONVERTIBLE

While in the South, we visited other Southern historically Black colleges and universities. We took road trips to Atlanta, meeting colleagues I had only known by mail and phone and viewing their art collections after being introduced to Tuskegee's. I tried to soak up Black history and culture in real life, which I had only known through books.

I was fascinated by the lush countryside with rivers, streams, and green hills. So, I asked my mother to ship my black rag-top red convertible to Tuskegee, and she did. When the truck carrying my little car pulled up to my house, neighbors came out of their front doors or pulled back their drapes to see what was happening in their neighborhood. They were astonished that I would send for this little car because almost everyone had bigger, better, and longer luxury automobiles. They explained by saying, "Well, you know, she's from California."

Most of our road trips were an hour away to Atlanta, where I visited friends at Clark Atlanta and Spelman universities. In addition, I drove to Hampton University to see its art collection and visit other colleagues. Then, one summer, we drove to Fisk University, where my husband and I had humanities fellowships.

Driving from Tuskegee Institute in Alabama to Fisk University in Nashville took about five-and-a-half hours in a red rag-top VW convertible with two young boys, a toddler, and a black Labrador retriever. I'd been busy closing the school year for my art students and my three children after having a course load of three classes and the responsibility of researching the school's art collection. My eyes were the first to see some of the collection documents for at least four decades. That summer, I almost forgot that my husband and I had applied for a Humanities Teaching Fellowship from the National Endowment for Humanities. Although surprised that we both got the positive news, packing up the kids and dog for a two-month stay in Nashville was daunting.

With the car packed to its roof, along with our clothes, we managed to squeeze Christopher's car seat in the center of the back seat between the older boys, Myles and Cary, who hovered around him to make room for our full-grown dog, Todo, who shared the floor with Christopher's small collapsible stroller.

It was the summer, and Nashville simmered as we rolled into the city, headed for Fisk University faculty housing. No faculty were around. They had enough sense to leave the summer heat for less sweltering locations. Ceramicist and printmaker Earl J. Hooks was the only one who remained; he served as caretaker of the art department, where I would spend most of my time reviewing their archives and viewing pieces in the collection.

We spent significant time in the libraries, my husband researching the Fisk Jubilee Singers and me the portrayal of Black musicians in American art. We found daycare for the children, ages one, five, and seven. We enrolled the two older children into an integrated camp. But one son came home and told us that a White child called him a Nigger. It reminded me of Countee Cullen's poem "Incident." I learned it in a college class on Black literature taught by my Martinican professor.

"Incident"

Once riding in old Baltimore,
Heart-filled, head-filled with glee,
I saw a Baltimorean
Keep looking straight at me.

Now I was eight and very small,
And he was no whit bigger,
And so I smiled, but he poked out
His tongue, and called me, "Nigger."

I saw the whole of Baltimore
From May until December.
Of all the things that happened there
That's all that I remember.[1]

—Countee Cullen

This poem about racism and lost innocence was a wake-up call for my sons and me. At Tuskegee, they lived a privileged life among people who cared for their well-being and development. They were celebrated for their progress and encouraged to excel. It was a place where they were loved.

Their experiences reminded me of how Southern Black rural teachers committed to teaching and delivering education to the masses of disenfranchised Black students. It reminded me of the tasks and challenges Booker T. Washington embraced as he opened his school to hundreds of the newly freed enslaved.

Even with all the new experiences, Tuskegee offered my family a protective atmosphere; this brush with the reality of racism colored our experiences in the South. Indeed, as they grew into young men, they remembered it. In the mid-1980s, we left Tuskegee for Los Angeles. While working in LA as the founding curator of art on staff for the

My father (Ulysses Weldon LeFalle) with Myles LeFalle Collins, my
eldest son, upon returning to LA from Tuskegee.

California African American Museum, I traveled to Shreveport to see
my grandparent's two-story house, but only the first floor remained.
I observed vacant grassy lots with prickly longleaf pines separating
the few homes on Talbot Street. The pine needles George Washington
Carver weaved during his years at Tuskegee were perfect for weaving pine baskets. Blackberry vines had long recaptured areas where
the two-story dairy barn once housed cows. They reminded me of the
blackberry vines in my childhood Los Angeles backyard that grew in all
their wildness on the side of the garage and tool shed. My mother had
us pick those blackberries, just as she had picked them for her mother to
make a cobbler. But blackberries also brought memories of Mom's sister
Wilma and her blackberry adventures that ultimately ended in tragedy.

In the distance, a row of wire fencing covered by purple morning glo-
ries was a footprint from the past. Developers planted indistinguishable
brick houses around a small but open pasture on every available inch
of barren land. While some community structures like Black churches,
benevolent society buildings, and schools remained in place, the private
enterprise dairy was no longer a visible part of the landscape. I could

visualize the dairy because of my Aunt Beaut's stories. She was the last sibling living in Shreveport; she never left.

Sitting on the sofa of her newer brick home, I listened to her stories once or twice and envisioned walking along the path from the back door of my mother's house as the smells of hay that had carpeted the dairy floor filled my nostrils. Sneezing all the time, this girl from Los Angeles struggled to find her grandfather among the cow stalls, manure, and steel milk cans. The dairy was gone, but the big fig tree my mother described in the front yard was still there. They can live to be one hundred years old.

> "I waited all summer long to pick the ripe black figs from the big old tree at the front gate."
>
> —AUNT BEAUT

It was there before Grandpa cleared the woodlands for their family home. Folks said it was the only tree he saved from that former wilderness. Then, Aunt Beaut took me to her pantry, and there they were, rows and rows of neatly packed figs lined up in little jars.

In 2009, my sister Deborah took our mother back to her family home in Louisiana. At the abandoned house, Mom said, "There's the fig tree." Half of its branches loaded with figs in the front yard reached over a chain-linked fence separating the yard from a well-worn footpath along the street.

> "There was a giant fig tree behind the barn and another one in the front yard of the house. The tree out back of the barn was for the family, but the one at the corner of the front yard was for anyone who wanted to pick figs."
>
> —MOM

While we were there, two men walked up the path to the tree and began doing what neighbors had done for decades: gather figs. When late summer rolled around, everyone understood it was fig-picking time to share the season's gifts. Picking, processing, and preserving figs was a ritual that connected extended family members who had migrated from points in Louisiana to California cities and to folks who stayed in the rural and semirural areas of the South.

"We lived a few steps from each other. Aunt Phoebe (Teet) had fig trees [in her yard]. She'd have fig-preserving parties where people in the neighborhood came over to pick and preserve the figs. We'd have enough preserves for the entire winter."

—COUSIN VIOLET (GRANDMA'S SISTER PHOEBE'S DAUGHTER)

California and Texas produce most of the commercial crops of figs, but growing up in my Los Angeles neighborhood, someone always had a fig tree ripe for picking. I remember Aunt Lizzetta having one in her backyard in LA.

FIGS OUT BACK

It was the fig-picking season in the San Francisco Bay Area, where I've lived for many years. I was ready to pick the sweet, plump fruit from behind my mother's cottage in San Jose and turn them into to-die-for jars of fig preserves. I had been writing all summer but was still behind on my writing projects. "Do you ever catch up with anything?" I asked myself. Then, I got the call. "The figs are ready," said my sister, Deborah. "You have to pick them this Saturday, or the birds will leave you with nothing but stems," she continued. It was figs or writing. Weighing my two options, I chose figs. As important as writing was to me, childhood memories of a bowl of fresh figs on my Aunt Lizzetta's solid oak round table with lion claws at the end of the legs were more appealing to my taste buds.

After a quick shower, still buttoning up my shirt, I grabbed an apple and headed out my front door. As the sun's rays filtered through the treetops, I drove down my driveway, turned toward Highway 101, and headed south to San Jose. What a perfect Saturday morning. A cloudless blue sky replaced an endless bank of low-hanging dark gray clouds that had me wondering if I would ever see the sun again.

The seductive figs lured me out into the sun, tired or not. I drove along the undulating highway past cows, barns, wild oaks, and bales of hay. In late August, the weekend traffic was surprisingly light. It was too early for the late Friday night revelers, who were likely still sprawled among their bed sheets. I pulled into the driveway of Deborah's English Tudor home and headed to Mom's cottage in the back. Mom had moved to her San Jose "Granny Cottage" from San Francisco in her mid-seventies. Now, at ninety, it was her place of solace and comfort. No more flights of stairs, traffic horns, and dark passages tunneled under the two-story Victorian building and up the brick stairway into the light of the small, lushly planted backyard. She lived in one of the two flats built after the 1906 San Francisco earthquake. Her sister, Lilly, owned the building and had lived in the upper unit since 1942, the great exodus days when crowds of Black people migrated from the gentle hills of northern Louisiana to the vertical Northern California city pierced by the morning fog and the smell of the Pacific Ocean.

San Jose is in a sunny valley, where fruit orchards once grew in the large lots of Deborah's Willow Glen neighborhood. When most of the newer homeowners who poured out of the Silicon Valley tech industry moved in, they changed the character of the quaint community, digging out the remainder of citrus and avocado orchards, extending or tearing down modest houses, and building monster homes. But Deborah, a longtime resident, had other plans. She had a Granny Cottage built with the same-pitched roof as her house, and I was on my way to visit Mom.

I pulled into the driveway and walked back to the cottage. "Morning, Mom," my voice rang out in a singsong fashion, my usual loud tone when addressing my mother, who refuses to wear her hearing aid. "Good morning, Liz," Mom said, calling me by my nickname rather than my given name of Lizzetta. She pulled back her white cotton panels from one corner of her front window, took a few steps to unlock two locks, and opened the door. The smell of strong black coffee wafted throughout her small cottage. A coffee drinker all her adult life, she took it black, saying, "I want to taste the coffee." While she poured me a cup, I opened her back door to take a quick look around the corner of the cottage at the fig tree.

My eyes followed its outstretched branches that spanned the distance from Mom's cottage to the property's back fence, about twenty feet. The scent of the purple Mission figs fueled my appetite as they hung from the tree like Christmas ornaments. I reached for a low-hanging fig and, holding it by the stem, parted it in half and sucked the succulent magenta contents into my mouth. As my tongue moved around the luscious fig, I thought of faraway places: Middle Eastern deserts with tall fan palms and caravans of camels making their way across distances where I could see no end. Unfortunately, there was no time for one of my frequent travel daydreams. So, instead, I went back inside the cottage and sat across from my mother at her round wooden dining table, painted white and draped with a floral tablecloth. It was not quite Aunt Lizzetta's clawed foot oak table, but it stimulated my imagination of my aunt and the stories about her youth. Mom and I chatted over buttered toast and strong coffee about the figs and Mom's parents' Lakeside Dairy, where her mother picked figs and made preserves. All the while, I wished I had some of those preserves to dress my warm toast.

As we finished our breakfast, Deborah knocked on the front door, and I went to greet her. She said, "Let's get going before the sun heats the sky." I had become too relaxed at Mom's table. So, I grabbed my garden gloves and said, "You're right, it's fig-picking time. See you later, Mom," and I left her to finish her breakfast. A tall ladder waited for me as I walked to the fig tree. I stood there gazing at the towering tree with dark purple orbs mingled among the hand-like leaves. Then I heard the tapping sound of Mom's walking cane, which assured me she had followed close behind, not one to be left out of anything, especially on this fig-picking day. When I scaled the narrow ladder, my sister stood below holding baskets while my mother directed my hand into the tree with her carved walking cane. "Liz, get those there; they're ready to pick," she said. "Okay, Mom," I said as I reached for the figs, picked them, and gingerly dropped the sweet purple ones into the baskets, careful not to bruise any. The dark color of the Mission figs made them easy to see, but then Mom pointed to large clumps in the center of the tree. Deborah had already picked figs on the outside branches of the tree, so the center was still loaded with figs, leaves, and probably creatures that I did not see. It was an area she avoided and left for me, but I was not ready to extend my arm into the dreaded center of the tree either. Then I heard my fearless mother. "Liz, get into the center. That's where the ripe figs are," straining her aged vocal cords to get my attention. I turned around and saw an expression on her face that I recognized from my days of encountering spiders while picking apricots and lemons from our backyard trees in Los Angeles. "Don't be afraid," she said, as I felt reduced to my childhood days. Being an adult about it, I reached into the center of the tree where she knew I could quickly fill my baskets, get out of there, and down the ladder. I prayed all the while that a spider wouldn't drop onto my extended arm, or I'd reach for the fruit and discover a spider's hiding place. "Peace be still," I remembered my mother saying, a call for calm amid fear. I kept saying it to the spiders, who undoubtedly occupied the same tree space as me. My call rewarded me for peace and stillness as I tossed clump after clump of figs to my sister to load the baskets until they were full to their brims. I looked down at all the dark teardrop shapes and gazed above, saying thank you, acknowledging the help of an unseen power that got me through the fig-picking ordeal spider-free.

I had picked enough figs to eat fresh, share, and preserve. It was a perfect fig-harvesting day and late morning as the sun heated the landscape. I still had time to drive home before the crush of Saturday sightseers hit the road north to the wine country. I didn't need any traffic jams with my carload of fresh figs. I filled up the trunk of my car and chatted with Deborah and Mom. Neither was into canning nor preserving, but they held high expectations for my fig preserves, praised throughout my family. I was the only one to keep the tradition of preserving figs alive, and everybody was expecting to have a jar or two or three.

I gave goodbye kisses all around and rubbed my mother's white silken hair, which became straight in her old age, before pressing my cheek against hers. "Bye, Mom, I love you," I said, giving her a big hug. Then, driving away, I glanced back at Mom in my rearview mirror until I couldn't see her anymore. Although I try to remain upbeat and cheerful in her presence, each visit, I know one day will be the last time that we will see each other. But I also know that I keep our fig-picking tradition alive to help her remember where she came from and the place and family that are no longer around her.

I'm always relieved to get past the central Bay Area and drive through the rolling hills of Sonoma County. Although it was a somewhat hectic morning, picking the figs was the easy part. My tasks were washing, laying them out to dry, and finding space in my full refrigerator. I won't lie; I was tired from rising too early on Saturday from a late night of writing. Driving two hours to San Jose from Santa Rosa and back, climbing the narrow ladder, reaching for the figs, frightful that I might encounter a spider, and leaving my mother behind was exhausting enough. I still had an hour of driving as I saw an onslaught of day-trippers hit the road going north. I started thinking about how figs came to California. I remembered a few fun facts about figs, thinking about them to keep me awake on the road. First, they originated in northern Asia Minor and spread throughout the Mediterranean with the Greeks and Romans. Finally, Spanish Franciscan missionaries brought figs to California in 1520. The black variety best known in California is Mission figs from that history. This sounded plausible to me as I finally turned into my driveway. Making it home, I knew I couldn't do much more that day but wash and dry the figs.

So here I am, overwhelmed with fresh figs, too many to preserve alone. I wanted a fig-preserving partner who shared my affinity for figs and one who understood the culture of the fig-picking time. I knew the right person. He lived with me; it was my husband, Willie. His mother, aunts, and cousins picked figs and made preserves every season. It was a perfect opportunity to invoke family stories because we knew family and friends who believed making fig preserves was more than creating a tasty treat for cold winter mornings. Processing and preserving figs was a ritual that connected us to our extended family members who had migrated from Louisiana to California and those who stayed home in the South. While making fig preserves, we talked about how they made a life for themselves under the strict segregation laws of Jim Crow and how they still built sustainable and thriving communities despite them. Rituals are essential in our lives, especially when conjuring family stories and friends.

For us, canning figs was an act of remembrance. But it would take more than remembrances to get Willie to join me in preparing the figs for preserving and sealing them into the clean, steaming hot glass jars with metal lids. So, I enticed him with my grandmother's buttermilk biscuit recipe to sweeten the invitation. Aside from canning the figs, we'd make the flaky biscuits like my grandmother made each morning, dressing them with butter churned from the dairy cows' milk spread across each opened half. My grandmother topped the biscuits with an ample dollop of homemade fig preserves from the family's fig tree outback. The idea to offer biscuits as an incentive came from talking to Uncle Angus, my mother's last living brother.

"Mom would serve us two big pans of biscuits every morning, and two big pans of cornbread for dinner, without fail."
—UNCLE ANGUS

So, with the addition of fluffy biscuits, it seemed very fitting to continue the tradition of canning figs for preserves from the tree in the back of my mother's cottage in San Jose, just as her mother had done from the fig tree at the rear of the Lakeside Dairy barn.

Willie and I got up early the following day, pulled out our Dutch oven, and filled it with figs and plenty of sugar, the Southern way, to protect fig preserves from decay and ensure their sweetness. Boil, rinse in cold water, rest the figs, boil a sugary syrup until thick, and season with sliced lemon rounds, then pour over the batch of cooked figs— Willie knew the routine after witnessing his mother, aunts, and cousins prepare the figs for preserves season after season. Also, from a small farming community, his knowledge was from a deep well of first-hand experiences among generations of his family members. The process reinforced my respect for his knowledge of Black folk culture. I learned from family members who were part of the exodus out of the South, who reinterpreted their gardens in Los Angeles, San Francisco, and Seattle based on that cultural knowledge from ancestors.

I remember why I also picked figs, described in some cultures as the fruit of the Gods. Having them around is also a part of religious life among faiths. I don't know if fig trees and their fruit had this associative meaning for my ancestors, but I like figs for more tactile reasons. I want to bite them straight from the tree and squeeze the sweet mushiness out of their skins while others, like my husband, pop the whole fig, skin and all, into his mouth. Either way, there is something very satisfying when I hear the crackle and feel the texture of tiny seeds in my mouth. When I pass a fig tree or encounter figs in produce market stalls, memories of figs flood my memory.

After processing the figs, filling the jars, and sealing them with screw-on tops, we placed them in a clean, dry place to chill overnight. We cleaned the kitchen so we wouldn't wake to a trail of ants the following day. We were so tired that we seemed to fall asleep immediately after hitting our crisp, percale bed sheets.

This was one of the rituals that played out repeatedly, an essential part of ruralizing our lives, mainly because those memories conjure family stories. But processing the figs wasn't the end of the story. Next, I had to make a fresh batch of biscuits. Grandma made great pans of them for her large family each morning. My mother didn't make them, but Aunt Lizzetta did, and we all gathered at her house to watch her fold over the dough and bake and butter the biscuits straight from the oven. Aunt Lizzetta brewed black coffee in her percolator for her and my mother, and we had milk.

"At home, it was a big round dark table where everyone would eat on special occasions. I can't remember the chairs. Most of the time, we would sit at the long farm table in the kitchen. It almost ran the length of the kitchen. Papa made long benches that ran along each side of the table. We all sat there and ate breakfast, lunch, and dinner."

—MOM

"For dinner, we had to wait for Dad to come to the table before saying the blessing, and we would bless the table every night. After that, he would most likely be in the barn tidying up, and we had to wait for him to come out of the barn before we could eat. It was a table of twelve of us, and Sister Mabel would serve the food. I called Mabel the 'Issuer Outter' because she would serve the food and make the plates."

—UNCLE ANGUS

With these memories on my mind the following day, Willie and I went straight to the kitchen to make biscuits, daydreaming as we folded over the dough. Baked fresh and buttered, we brewed strong black coffee and dressed the hot treat with our fig preserves. I sat at my dining table and stared out the window at the rising sun, thinking this is why I picked figs. Each time I wondered why I ever began fig preserving in the first place, I already knew the answer. As a child, I remember my aunts and uncles returning to Los Angeles from Shreveport with their suitcases loaded with little glass jars of homemade preserves and gifts from family and friends in the South. I thought of Aunt Lizzetta in LA bringing biscuits and jam to the round table, where my feet barely reached the floor below. The bright sun from the window behind me warmed my back. My aunt and mother started talking about Lakeside Dairy as we began to eat. I listened intensely—a warm heat radiated from the kitchen oven, still warm from baking the biscuits. I felt like I was back at Lakeside Dairy, warmed by the hearth's crackling fireplace in the big farmhouse kitchen. I also learned many years later that the round oak table that Aunt Lizzetta had in her living room was a smaller version of a large dark wood table that stood in the dining room of the Bates family home. Although the memories of the dairy come only through the stories told by my family members, they are rich ones; I hear them over and over until I recite them as my own.

Continuing the gift of sharing, I invited my artist friend, Mildred Howard, over to preserve figs. She wanted to celebrate her birthday by doing a different activity with each of her friends. She also brought strawberries and tomatoes. Although we both had canned separately in our kitchens, we never had canned fruit together, so this was a perfect opportunity to work side by side, canning what we loved. As I thought about it, the appeal of canning with my friend became more attractive because while we were both art professionals (artist and curator), we also shared similar family backgrounds.

So, processing and canning figs was more than creating a tasty treat for cold winter mornings. The process and ingestion of figs was an act of remembrance. This ritual connected us to our long-gone family members who migrated from points in East Texas and northwest Louisiana to California. My friend remembers her introduction to figs.

"I didn't like figs growing up. I tried them on and off as a child, but I only liked cooked figs. It's different now. I like them both ways. What interests me is the variety of figs that are available now. My oldest brother had a fig tree in his backyard, the ones with the deep purple peel. I was fascinated by the purple color against the light green inner edge and the reddish center of the fig. I can remember picking them for my mother. I'd open them and it seemed like the center had millions of seeds. It's funny how the memories linger. I learned to can from watching my mother and my grandmother, Lulu."

—MILDRED HOWARD, ARTIST

❈

Figs. Illustration by author.

FIG PRESERVES

Hands-on time: 1 hour 30 mins
Total time: 5 hours 35 mins
Yield: 4 to 6 pint-sized jars

Ingredients:
    8–10 cups small, firm but ripe figs
    2 cups granulated sugar
    1-inch knob of fresh ginger peeled and diced (or dried)
    1 small fresh lemon, thinly sliced
    1 juice of 1 additional fresh lemon
    1 cup water

Preparation:
    Layer the figs with lemon slices, sugar, sliced ginger, and lemon juice
    in a wide, heavy-bottomed, nonreactive pot. Cover and refrigerate
    for at least 4 hours or overnight.

Add the cup of water the next day and cover the pot with a lid. Bring the fig mixture to a simmer over medium heat. Turn the figs down to low and slow cook, covered for 1 hour. Observe. After the figs have cooked covered for 1 hour, vent the lid and cook for another 30 minutes with the top vented (or until the figs are translucent and the syrup has thickened). Transfer the fig mixture (with the lemon and ginger) to sterilized jars and refrigerate or process for 5 minutes in a water-bath canner to store on the shelf.

Notes:
When you load up your jars, leave the lemon and ginger in the mixture. They will add candied flavor.

After processing the figs, filling the jars, and sealing them with screw-on tops, we placed them in a clean, dry place to chill overnight.

EVERY MORNING BUTTERMILK BISCUITS

I call them Every Morning Buttermilk Biscuits because my grand-mother, like so many women during her time, got up early to bake fresh biscuits for their families every morning. The recipe had to be easy, with few ingredients for farming families.

Hands-on time: 30 minutes
Total time: 45 minutes
Yield: 12 to 14 biscuits

Ingredients:
   1 cup chilled buttermilk
   ½ cup cold grated butter (1 stick)
   2½ cups flour
   4 tsp. baking powder
   ½ tsp. baking soda
   1 tsp. salt

Preparation:
   Preheat oven to 475°F. Add all dry ingredients together in a large mixing bowl and whisk. Make a well in the center of the dry mixture

Every Morning Buttermilk Biscuits.

and add one stick of grated butter. Mix well (hands are best), add buttermilk, and mix again. The mixture will be sticky. Turn onto a floured board and pat edges together to form a rectangle. Roll the dough until it is about 9 inches long. Take each end of the rectangle and fold it into the center from each side. Then, fold it in half. Roll out the dough again; it should be about 5/8 inch thick. Repeat rolling each end to the center, then folding over. Roll with the rolling pin again, repeating this process 2 to 3 more times. It's like you are making puff pastry, but this will not be as light. After the last rotation, roll the dough to cut your biscuits. It should be about ½ inch thick. Use a small glass or mason jar if you don't have a biscuit cutter. Cut the biscuits. Place them on a cookie sheet covered with parchment paper. Brush the tops with butter before putting them in the oven. Bake for 15 minutes. Remove from the oven and with more butter, jam, preserves, or syrup.

Wild Plums. Illustration by author.

WILD PLUM JAM

Hands-on time: 20 minutes
Total time: 20 minutes
Yield: 8–10 jars

Ingredients:
    2–3 lbs. wild plums
    2/3 cup of sugar
    ½ medium lemon, zested
    2 Tbsp. lemon juice
    water to cover plums
    ¼ tsp. ginger (grate fresh or powder), optional

Preparation:
    Wash plums and place them in a boiler with water, sugar, lemon juice, lemon zest, and ginger. Heat the pan to a rapid boil for ten minutes, then reduce the heat to a simmer. The plums will cook down and break apart. Turn off the heat and remove to a cold burner to cool.

When cool, remove the seeds. Taste for desired flavor and return to the heat. Cook until the consistency is spreadable. Store in the refrigerator if you are not processing the preserves in glass canning jars. It should last for about two weeks. Serve on hot buttered biscuits or toast, using a clean knife or spoon each time you dip into the jar.

CONCLUSION

AFTER RESEARCHING THE DAIRY, INCLUDING THE RECORDS GATHERED by family members, I revisited the home site in 2016. The present vacant and deteriorating house had no resemblance to the home where my mother and her family lived. The portion of the house that remained had inexpensive fiber cement siding. My mother remembered salespeople trolling neighborhoods, convincing homeowners with few resources that this was better for their home than the old cedar siding that had to be maintained by painting. Judging from the miss-cuts around the windows and doors, whoever put the siding on the former Bates house was someone other than a carpenter. "Handmade" is an adequate description in the most derisive sense. Also, the new owners removed the second story of the house. The fig tree in the front yard remained the one recognizable part of the home site. Older and newer brick homes lined Talbot Street, and the dairyland fields that once led to the lake disappeared.

A few blocks away, old brick structures of the once-bustling Texas Avenue business district stood like ghosts of a past era. I drove up to Grandma's sister Jane's shotgun house, which she used to rent to a preacher. Wood, gray with age, stood as a signature to a bygone area. The influx of Haitians initially influenced the architecture in France's Louisiana. Thousands of free people of color migrated to New Orleans after the Haitian (then Saint-Domingue) Revolution in 1804. The home sites in New Orleans, especially in and around the French Quarter, were limited by lot size and had more embellishments than those in northwest Louisiana. Most of the ones in the northwest didn't have decorative finials. They were very plain in comparison to the ones in New Orleans.

Great-Aunt Jane, Grandma's sister's shotgun house.

My people told me that the label shotgun house described the struc-ture. If you stood at the front door and aimed your shotgun straight ahead through the back door, the pellets would exit the house on the other side. Some houses don't have a hallway for those pellets to travel through. But Grandpa built his house that way, but with more rooms, which may be especially true for northern Louisiana. But I see fewer and fewer of these houses each time I go. The families that had since moved on became a part of that exodus out of the South. The structure seems to depend on the builder's skills and the doors' alignment. Some multistory houses, like the Bates home, were also built on the shot-gun model.

"We lived in a two-story house at 2102 Talbot Street. Pastureland was in the back and to the side of the house, and this is where my father ran his business, Lakeside Dairy. We had cows and chickens, a mule, and a bull; and we grew vegetables. There was a wide hallway down the middle of our house, and you could see a straight shot from the front door to the back door. We had a large kitchen with a farmhouse table and a separate dining room too."

—ELOISE

Aunt Jane's shotgun house is still standing. She moved out of it many years ago and began renting it to traveling preachers, but it has been vacant for decades. It reminds me of an old decaying tree that will eventually fall into the earth.

Grandpa Angus died in the winter of 1935, confirmed by a death certificate. Was his birthright a constant reminder of his questionable beginnings? Was his birth the result of a drunken indiscretion or violent act, or was it the result of a consensual secret romantic encounter, an encounter that had long been illegal? Shreveport's waterways were just as well known for the secret social and racial rendezvous of waves of immigrants up from the infamous Port of New Orleans as they were for carrying bales of cotton and sugar cane. For this reason, Grandpa Angus was very protective of his family, especially his girls. So, after years of combing through family history and coming up empty, I guess it was time for my Aunt Lilly to reveal the family secret.

His conception was considered immoral and dangerous. It threatened the lives of the Black person in a liaison because Whites could explain it as a youthful fling or temporary indiscretion. Though frowned upon, a sanctioned rendezvous by a White man with a Black woman was common so his wife or fiancé would not have to endure his repeated sexual advances. A proper Southern lady was there to bear his children, not to engage endlessly in sex, but her husband could. The evidence of miscegenation is in the historical to contemporary numbers of multi-brown-toned Black people. It could have been the other way around—a White woman and a Black man—a hated and deadly combination then, but back then, that surely meant his death.

I wonder if this reality of the South weighed heavily on my grandfather's consciousness or tormented him. Did it pull him down physically, causing him to have a constant but thoughtful, stern gaze as if his mind was off somewhere else as he did his daily chores as a dairy farmer? Was this hulking figure of a man troubled by a past he didn't understand? As Black people in the New World, we know that history is elusive to us, and the subtle details of our lineage leave many open wounds.

We share a group identity and tonalities mixed with Blackness, but what of the personal stories that often lie hidden behind veils of shame? We see our colorful selves knowing that we didn't just happen to come in these varying degrees of black, brown, tan, and cream—the blue-black, ash-browns, and redbone hues that signal our movement in and out of various New World ethnic communities. How they came to be are the kinds of secrets kept for generations. Did Grandpa even know, did he care, or did he accept his lot as the consequence of history or something he could do little about during his lifetime? Whatever happened, he did his best with his identity, but Angus was a rare name for a Black male in the US (although there are now four in my family alone).

A few years after his death, my mother and aunts described a White man from San Francisco who came to the house. He asked my grandmother about my grandpa. Aunt Lilly always mentioned the "old man's" name across the pasture in the context of Grandpa's family. The "old man's" family, whom Uncle Angus described, came from a family who had owned much of the land, including the dairy property—a former plantation. Families did not always reveal their secrets back then. Still, suspicion has forever suggested that the family name had something to do with Grandpa Angus's father and Lakeside Dairy. But the story varies. Aunt Lilly, one of the oldest siblings who looked most like Grandpa, with cream-colored skin, gray eyes, and silken hair, settled in San Francisco, the city of the mysterious visitor. However, she never revealed all she knew except that Grandpa's father was Italian. She lived until she was one hundred, taking the rest of Grandpa's story to her grave.

He could have been based on the clients who purchased his milk products and lived close to the dairy. But who was the man Uncle Angus described as Flournoy, who lived not far from the Bateses? The mystery continues.

By the late 1950s, only one Bates sibling remained in Louisiana. In 1957, Aunt Lizzetta took a train to Shreveport to bring Grandma to Los Angeles to live among most of her children. Grandma, although frail, did not want to leave the house of memories that her husband and partner in the dairy business had built. Yet she decided to come, but she transitioned just days before boarding the train. Family members were devastated, and Aunt Lizzetta returned to LA alone.

"I had gone to Shreveport [from Los Angeles] to bring her here to stay with me. So that morning before we were supposed to leave, she said, 'Take me out on the front porch so I can look over the countryside.' And I carried her on the front porch to the front steps, brought her back in, and sat her in the chair in the dining room. And she gasped for breath and was gone right then and there. Now, this is the day before we're supposed to get ready to come back to California. She did not want to come to California and leave her home. So, I'm thinkin' when she went on that front porch, she went there to pray and [ask] that the Heavenly Father would take her on, so she wouldn't have to come back to California. Honey, she did not want to come to California."

—AUNT LIZZETTA

I began this narrative about my grandparents' Lakeside Dairy and stopped and started many times. But the dairy always had a way of disrupting my writing plans. I moved to other topics, but after meeting with my mother or another family member, I felt compelled to return to their memories about the dairy and record them as relatable to others. I chose storytelling because it was the medium by which I received my family's memories.

I imagined Jersey and Holstein cows in the green pastures of northwest Louisiana, the smell of fresh hay in the barn shared with the milking stations where warm white milk flowed from cow udders into sterilized galvanized containers each morning. As a child growing up in Los Angeles, my mother's family's memories stamped the stories into my head. My childhood romance with dairy life waned as I reached adulthood and interviewed my mother and her siblings about being involved in the dairy business. I realized that dairy work was hard, dusty, and not for me. The stories became a lesson in environmental challenges to Black farmers and sustainability and how they overcame a system stacked against them. These lessons rang true for anyone faced with life's challenges and the will to move through them.

Lakeside Dairy moments affected my journey through life's seasons, encouraging me to drink in the natural environment, taste its offerings, and work its gardens to sustain my body and soul. My grandparents' entrepreneurial spirit moved me to live a whole life, be myself, follow my path, and not limit myself by what others say about me. The stories about the dairy were a coming-of-age toolbox at different points in my young life, reminding me to seek knowledge and beauty in ordinary places, often among ordinary and extraordinary people.

My mother used to state emphatically, "We lived in town," meaning they were not country folk. But I wondered how she could live in the town with all the cows and other farm animals. What did that life mean

Bates siblings in LA: Uncle Angus, Aunt Lilly, Aunt Lena, my mother,
Eloise, Aunt Lula, Aunt Phoebe, and Aunt Lizzetta.

for those who migrated from small towns effaced by rural agricultural environments? They retained the character of their social and familial life, which grew in a pastoral context. The Allendale community was a village within the larger city of Shreveport. Living in town was relative to the proximity of other markers, cultural definitions, and historical points. The house was in line with other homes on Talbot Street, but the back stretched well into the distance, almost to the lake, and the front close to the Texas Avenue business section, the Black part of Shreveport. I realized that Lakeside Dairy was in town in Shreveport, Louisiana, yet out of it. It was the city-country combination, so desired in modern living. Mom's family members replicated their Allendale village in many small yet meaningful ways in their Los Angeles village. Their stories of country life on a working dairy, some humorous, most times cautionary, and full of life lessons, illustrated how the family navigated their way with joy and communion in the era of Jim Crow. They rose above what my great-grandmother called "the dark periods" of enslavement and its legacy that followed them west into the promise of continued growth and new possibilities. Although reinventing their lives in a place far from home, they held tight to the memories and practices that kept them whole and in their right minds.

After the dairy closed in 1943 and the dairy barns were no longer standing, school children, including my third cousins, took a shortcut past the house where grandmother still lived and searched for coins where the barns once stood.

"We used to dig around in the dirt where the barn was looking for coins, and we found some."

—COUSIN MARSHALL MAE

ACKNOWLEDGMENTS

FIRST, I THANK THE CLOSE AND DISTANT FAMILY MEMBERS WHO NUR-
tured my interest in giving them a voice in *Seasons at Lakeside Dairy*.
Their personal stories and memories are at the crux of this book, and
they illustrate the value of recording family stories as verbal cultural
artifacts. The ephemera gathered from different family members support the storytelling.

Sincerely thanks to Aunt Lizzetta and Lilly for their collections of
photographs and other ephemera, and to Aunt Janice (Beaut), her
daughter Anita, and Anita's daughter, Shonda, who held onto ephemera
on the dairy, and sent it to my sister Deborah. Thank you to Deborah
for sharing the many papers that supported the diary's existence with
me when official Louisiana records ignored it. These dated documents
confirm how the dairy's history is connected to Black historical events
from 1907 to 1943. Additionally, thank you Lizzetta Lebeau Douglas
and Noelle Lebeau for sharing their mother, Aunt Phoebe's photo albums. Also, thank you to my cousin Michelle Flowers-Taylor for her
story about Aunt Alice, a dressmaker and designer. Thank you to Hardy
"Pat" Bates, Uncle David's son in Waskom, Texas, for sharing photos of
his father, especially one that places Uncle David on the Bates dairy with
the lake in the background. Also, thank you to cousins Linda, Michael,
Violet, and Cleo for sharing their photos and memories about the dairy
and Cousin Marshall Mae for sharing Great-Grandma Lilly Daisy Morris Davis's autobiography *Life Sketches* with the family.

My in-person interviews began years before I even thought of writing this book. They were on visits with my aunts and uncles, especially
aunts Lizzetta, Lilly, and Alice. I'd also queried uncles Angus and Booker
because of my interest in the dairy. I was living in Portland, Oregon,

when I decided to begin writing. I drafted a list of questions for Uncle Angus in Los Angeles. I asked my son, Myles, to visit with him and ask the questions in person. Myles graciously agreed, and Uncle Angus's answers clearly provided the workings of the dairy and the context for his family living and working to make it sustainable until the siblings began their westward migration. I'd also like to thank Randi Leffall and Francis Leffall Black, who shared their stories and photographs of my great-grandfather Jackson "Jack" Andrew Leffall on my father's side of our family. It helped me draw many connections to the context of Black lives in northeast Texas and northwest Louisiana. It also introduced me to how some Black people became landowners after freedom. I appreciate Dr. Edith Powell, the consultant for the George Washington Carver Papers at Tuskegee University, for providing me with a wealth of research images and documents from the collections of Booker T. Washington and Dr. George Washington Carver.

Black culinary authors helped me to anchor the foodways in Lakeside Dairy. I compared notes from family interviews with recipes in their books. *Seasons* is like the experiences of LA Black settlers that Toni Tipton Martin pens in her book *Jubilee: Recipes from Two Centuries of African American Cooking* (2019). While reading Martin's culinary books, I recalled my Aunt Lula's preparations of luncheons for wealthy families in Beverly Hills. I don't know where she learned to prepare and present such nuanced delicacies and aesthetically beautiful meals except at home for her mother's social club gatherings. I realized that some early Black chefs p: ...red similar meals, and then I thought of my Uncle Angus, too. He learned to cook initially by waiting tables and went from serving to learning to cook fine meals in a country club and hotel kitchens.

As I wrote about my aspirational grandparents and their approach to country cooking, I consulted Chef Edna Lewis's cookbooks, *The Edna Lewis Cookbook* (1972), *The Taste of Country Cooking* (1976), and *In Pursuit of Flavor* (1988). Even though my grandparents owned a dairy, macaroni and cheese was not a part of my grandparents' diet. Instead, their diet was heavily field-to-table, plant-based, and foraged from the subtropical environment of Louisiana, including the waterways where they lived. In Lewis's book, I looked for similarities to the recipes some of my aunts jotted down. They inevitably left out ingredients. Family members cooked red beans and rice, yellow cornmeal cornbread, sweet potato pone, collards, turnips, mustards, and other greens. Watching my mother cook in the kitchen taught me to taste as I go and trust my taste. I refer to recipes but create my own space with them, depending on the tastes I am after. Improvisation is my guide.

I also consulted Dr. Jessica B. Harris's *The Welcome Table: African American Heritage Cooking* (1995) and *High on the Hog: A Culinary Journey from Africa to America* (2011) as I reconstructed recipes based on my knowledge of ingredients and memory. Dr. Harris is central to the publication of this book. She read an excerpt from my book at a writing residency I attended at Renaissance House on Martha's Vineyard in 2018. Harris referred to it as a culinary memoir because of the many family stories of growing, harvesting, preparing, and eating foods from the dairy. She also revealed she was unaware of any written treatment that included Black dairy owners early in the twentieth century. I also discussed the book with Maida Owens, Folklife Program Director for the State of Louisiana, because of the dairy's location in Shreveport. She recommended I contact the University Press of Mississippi (UPM). When I told Dr. Harris about this recommendation, she asked me to write to the head editor at UPM, Craig Gill, and say to him at her suggestion she wanted me considered for her culinary series. Thank you to the staff at UPM for shepherding me through the publication process.

My breakthrough in writing was only possible with residencies that allowed me time and space to return to creative writing after a career in art curating and writing. So, I thank the resident opportunities and workshop leaders who paved the way for this publication. They include Atlantic Center for Arts, New Smyrna Beach, Florida with Honor Moore; Cat'Art Centre d'Art Contemporaine, La Forge Sainte Colombe sur l'Hers, France with Catherine Cordelle; Mesa Refuge, Point Reyes, California with Susan Tillett; Voices of Our Nations Arts (VONA), Berkeley, California, with Faith Adele; Renaissance House, Martha's Vineyard, Massachusetts, with Abigail McGrath and Jessica B. Harris; Anaphora Arts Writing Residency with Mahtam Shiferraw, Chris Abani, Phillip B. Williams, Marcelo Hernandez Castillo, and Airea D. Matthews; GenArts Virtual Poetry Fellowship, Santa Clara, California, with Keana Aguila Labra; South Porch Artists Residency, Summerville, South Carolina, with Brad Erickson and Brian Protheroe; and UCROSS Foundation Artists Fellowship, Clearmont, Wyoming, with Twani Shuler. Thank you to *The New Guard* for first publishing "Death's Fingers." More importantly, thank you to my mother, Eloise Bates LeFalle, husband and part-time editor of this book, Dr. Willie R. Collins, and three sons (Myles, Cary, and Christopher) for putting up with time away from them to write. Thank you for allowing me that space.

APPENDIX: BATES FAMILY TREE

THIS PARTIAL FAMILY TREE LISTS THE PRIMARY FAMILY MEMBERS MEN-tioned in the book, especially those quoted, to assist readers as they move through the chapters.

Grandfather: Angus Bates, Sr., 1870–1935

∞

Grandmother: Carrie Davis Bates, 1884–1957

Children
Leonard Bates, 1900–1979
Lena Bates Day, 1901–1982
David Morris "Bubba" Bates, 1905–1985
Janice Olivia "Beaut" Bates Gladney, 1907–1982
Lilly "Puddin" Bates Howard, 1909–2009
Lula Maude Bates Carter, 1912–1992
Lizzetta Bates Moore, 1913–2005
Mabel Bates Dabner, 1915–2005
Angus Bates, Jr., 1917–2014
Alice Alberta Bates Macklin, 1919–1992
Booker Taliaferro Bates, 1921–1970
Wilma Bates, 1923–1940
Eloise Bates LeFalle, 1924–2020
Phoebe Davis Bates Lebeau, 1927–2012

NOTES

INTRODUCTION

1. Dorothy Kilgallen, "Red Beans and Ricely, Yours," *Minneapolis Morning Tribune*, March 7, 1947, 6.

CHAPTER ONE: THE BATES SIBLINGS FIND A HOME IN LOS ANGELES

1. Toni Tipton Martin, *Jubilee: Recipes from Two Centuries of African American Cooking: A Cookbook* (New York: Clarkston Potter, 2019), 122; Hadley Meares, "Former Slave Rufus Estes Helped Teach America How to Cook," *LAist*, February 20, 2019, laist.com/news/la-history/rufus-estes-las-forgotten-pullman-chef-black-history.

2. David E. James, *The Sons and Daughters of Los: Culture and Community in L.A.* (Philadelphia: Temple University Press, 2003), 69.

3. Bette Yarborough Cox, *The Negro Directory of Black Los Angeles, CA, 1930–1931* (Los Angeles: California Eagle Pub. Co., 1930), 8–44.

4. Central Avenue Collaborative, "A Brief History of Central Avenue, Historic Central Avenue Los Angeles," www.nps.gov/nr/feature/afam/2010/Cover AfricanAmericans inLA.pdf; Cox, *Negro Directory*, 8–44.

5. Central Avenue Collaborative, "A Brief History."

6. Josh Sides, *L.A. City Limits: African American Los Angeles from the Great Depression to the Present* (Berkeley: U of California P, 2006), 34–35, 38, 44–45; Blacks continued to face overt White resistance and threats of violence that limited their residential mobility, although Black Angelinos led the nation in initiating lawsuits to eliminate racially restrictive covenants into the 1940s.

7. L. P. Boustan, "Was Postwar Suburbanization 'White Flight'? Evidence from the Black Migration," *Quarterly Journal of Economics* 125 (2010): 417–443.

8. Sides, *L.A. City Limits*.

9. Douglas Flamming, *Bound for Freedom: Los Angeles in Jim Crow America* (Berkeley: University of California Press, 2005), 296.

10. James Weldon Johnson, *The Autobiography of an Ex-Colored Man* (New York: Dover Publications, 1912).

11. James Baldwin, *The Price of the Ticket* (New York: Beacon Press, 1985), 660–61.

12. George Washington Carver, *Bulletin No. 5, 1903, Cow Peas*, George Washington Carver Collection, Tuskegee Institute University Archives, Tuskegee Institute, AL. They are now commonly known as black-eyed peas or field peas in the US; the cowpea was domesticated in Africa. It survived the Middle Passage from Africa to Jamaica with enslaved people and into the US, where it continued cultivation as a drought-resistant crop in the South. Some Blacks in south Los Angeles planted it in their urban farms.

13. Maida Owens, "Louisiana's Traditional Cultures: An Overview," in *Swapping Stories: Folktales from Louisiana*, ed. Carl Lindahl et al. (Jackson: University Press of Mississippi, 1997).

14. Louis R. Harlan, "Desegregation in New Orleans Public Schools During Reconstruction," *American Historical Review* 67, no.3 (1962): 663–75. https://doi.org/10.2307/1844107.

15. Robert Lowe, "The Strange History of School Desegregation," *College of Education Faculty Research and Publications* 88 (2004).

16. Gilles-Antoine Langlois, "River of Faith: 300 Years as a New Orleans Catholic Community," *Clarion Herald*, January 8, 2018; Gilles-Antoine Langlois, "Tricentennial Thursday: Make That Fleur de Lys, Not the Common Fleur de Lis," *Clarion Herald*, April 30, 2018, clarionherald.org/news/tricentennial-thursday-make-that-fleur-de-lys-not-the-common-fleur-de-lis. Also see Alice Dunbar-Nelson, "People of Color in Louisiana: Part II," *The Journal of Negro History* 2, no. 1 (1917): 51–58.

17. Psyche A Williams-Forson, *Building Houses out of Chicken Legs: Black Women, Food, and Power* (Chapel Hill: University of North Carolina Press, 2006).

CHAPTER TWO: A RESIDENCY IN A FRENCH VILLAGE

1. Michael Pollen, *The Botany of Desire: A Plant's-Eye View of the World* (New York: Random House Trade Paperbacks, 2001). See food charts for historically cultivated food regions.

CHAPTER THREE: SEASONS AT LAKESIDE DAIRY

1. John Andrew, "Our History: 1925 Allendale Fire Changed Shreveport," *Shreveport Times*, September 7, 2014, www.shreveporttimes.com/story/news/local/2014/09/07/history-allendale-fire-changed-shreveport/15267793/.

2. James L. McCorkle Jr., "Los Adeas," in *Handbook of Texas Online*, Texas State Historical Association, 1995, www.tshaonline.org/handbook/entries/los-adaes.

3. George Washington Carver, *No. 31, 1925 Experiment Station: How to Grow the Peanut and 101 Ways of Preparing it for Human Consumption*, George Washington Carver Collection, Tuskegee Institute University Archives, Tuskegee Institute, AL.

4. Paul Laurence Dunbar, "We Wear the Mask," in *The Complete Poems of Paul Laurence Dunbar* (New York: Dodd, Mead and Company, 1895). Retrieved online www.poetryfoundation.org/poems/44203/we-wear-the-mask.

5. Juan Battle and Earl Wright, "W. E. B. Du Bois's Talented Tenth: A Quantitative Assessment," *Journal of Black Studies* 32, no. 6 (2002): 654–72.

6. Raymond W. Smock, ed., "Booker T. Washington in Biographical Perspective." In *Booker T. Washington in Perspective: Essays of Louis R. Harlan*, 3–24. Jackson: University Press of Mississippi, 1988. Retrieved online from http://www.jstor.org/stable/j.ctt2tvj64.5.

7. "Shreveport Business League Meeting Best of Year," *Shreveport Times*, February 18, 1928, ephemera, Southern University Library Archive, Shreveport, LA, accessed June 8, 2022.

8. USDA "Black Farmers in America, 1865–2000," US Dept of Ag, Rural Business—Cooperative Service, RBS Research Report 194, 4–10, 19.

9. Dunbar-Nelson, "People of Color in Louisiana: Part II," 51–58.

10. Lesley Fleischman and Marcus Franklin, "Fumes across the Fence-Line: The Health Impacts of Air Pollution from Oil & Gas Facilities on African American Communities," NCAAP and Clean Air Task Force, November 2017, www.catf.us/wp content/uploads/2017/11/CATF_Pub_FumesAcrossTheFenceLine.pdf.

11. See William P. Jones, *The Tribe of Black Ulysses: African American Lumber Workers in the Jim Crow South* (Champaign: University of Illinois Press, 2005).

12. USDA "Black Farmers in America, 1865–2000," *US Dept of Ag, Rural Business—Cooperative Service*, RBS Research Report 194, 4–10, 19.

CHAPTER FOUR: WORKING THROUGH THE ICY WINTER DAYS AND NIGHTS

1. USDA, "Black Farmers," Carver, *No. 31*.

2. George Washington Carver, *No. 21 1911 Experiment Station: White &Color Washing with Native Clays from Macon Co., AL*, George Washington Carver Collection, Tuskegee Institute University Archives, Tuskegee Institute, AL.

3. Carver. *No. 21*.

4. US Census records and state census records will all yield the names and occupations of African Americans such as Henry Floke (or Florke), who owned an ice cream saloon in Kentucky in 1870.

5. Katherine Byers and Dennis Savaiano, "The Myth of Increased Lactose Intolerance in African Americans," *Journal of the American College of Nutrition* 24 (Dec. 2005): 569S–573S.

6. Y. Yang et al., "Favorite Foods of Older Adults Living in the Black Belt Region of the United States: Influences of Ethnicity, Gender, and Education," *Appetite* 63 (April 2013): 18–23.

7. National Association for the Advancement of Colored People. *Fourth Annual Report, January 1914*, W. E. B. DuBois Papers, MS 312, Special Collections and University Archives, University of Massachusetts Amherst, 51.

8. NCAAP, *Fourth Annual Report*; George Washington Carver, *No. 43 1942 Experiment Station: Nature's Garden for Victory & Peace*, George Washington Carver Collection, Tuskegee Institute University Archives, Tuskegee Institute, AL.

CHAPTER FIVE: SPRING PLANNING FOR THE NEXT YEAR

1. Carver, *No. 43*.

2. Carver, *No. 43*.

3. Mary Church Terrell, "The Progress of Colored Women," Address delivered before the National American Women's Suffrage Association, Washington, DC, February 18, 1898, E449 .D16 vol A., no. 13, Daniel Murray Pamphlet Collection and African American Pamphlet Collection, Library of Congress, Washington, DC. www.loc.gov/exhibits/odyssey/educate/terrell.htmlTerrellWritings,1972.

4. Terrell, "Progress"; Battle, "W. E. B. Du Bois's," 654–72.

5. National Park Service, *African American Heritage & Ethnology*, Park Ethnography Program, https://www.nps.gov/ethnography/aah/aaheritage/frenchama.htm.National Park Service. *The Oaks Tuskegee Institute National Historic Site*, Cultural Landscape Report. "Site History, The Oaks, Margaret Murray Washington Period (1915–1925).

6. National Park Service, *African American Heritage & Ethnology*.

7. David T. Beito, *From Mutual Aid to the Welfare State: Fraternal Societies and Social Services, 1890–1967* (Chapel Hill: University of North Carolina Press, 1999).

CHAPTER SEVEN: FALL RETURNS AND GRANDPA DIES IN EARLY DECEMBER

1. US States Census Records 1910, Fourth Ward, Shreveport, Caddo Parish, Louisiana, sheet 16.

2. "Black Americans in Congress: Introduction," Office of the Historian, History, Art & Archives, (Washington, DC: US House of Representatives, 2008), history.house.gov/Exhibitions-and-Publications/BAIC/Historical-Essays/Introduction/Introduction/.

3. Charles Siler, "A Commentary: African Cultural Retentions in Louisiana," *Folklife in Louisiana: Louisiana's Living Traditions*, www.louisianafolklife.org/LT/Articles_Essays/afri_cult_retent.html.

CHAPTER EIGHT: THE LEGACY AND HISTORICAL AND CULTURAL CONTEXT OF LAKESIDE DAIRY

1. Countee Cullen, "Incident," in *My Soul's High Song: The Collected Writings of Countee Cullen*, ed. Gerald Early (New York: Anchor Books, 1990).

BIBLIOGRAPHY

Andrew, John. "Our History: 1925 Allendale Fire Changed Shreveport." *Shreveport Times,* September 7, 2014. https://www.shreveporttimes.com/story/news/local/2014/09/07/history-allendale-fire-changed-shreveport/15267793/.

Baldwin, James. *The Price of the Ticket.* New York: Beacon Press, 1985.

"Ballyhoo." *Shreveport Times,* July 9, 1932. Southern University Shreveport Archives, Shreveport, Louisiana. Accessed, June 8, 2022.

Battle, Juan, and Earl Wright. "W. E. B. Du Bois's Talented Tenth: A Quantitative Assessment." *Journal of Black Studies* 32, no. 6 (2002): 654–72. doi.org/10.1177/002347020320060.

Beito, David T. *From Mutual Aid to the Welfare State: Fraternal Societies and Social Services, 1890–1967.* Chapel Hill: University of North Carolina Press, 1999.

"Black Americans in Congress: Introduction." Office of the Historian, History, Art & Archives. Washington, DC: US House of Representatives, 2008. history.house.gov/Exhibitions-and-Publications/BAIC/Historical-Essays/Introduction/Introduction/.

Brown, Audrey, and Erika Hill. *African American Heritage & Ethnography: A Self-Paced Training Resource.* Washington, DC: Ethnography Program, National Park Service, 2006. www.nps.gov/ethnography/aah/aaheritage/frenchama.html.

Boustan, L.P. "Was Postwar Suburbanization 'White Flight'? Evidence from the Black Migration." *Quarterly Journal of Economics* 125 (2010): 417–443.

Byers, Katherine, and Dennis Savaiano. "The Myth of Increased Lactose Intolerance in African Americans," *Journal of the American College of Nutrition* 24 (Dec. 2005): 569S–573S.

Carver, George Washington. "George Washington Carver to Miss. Liston and Budd." [1917], TIA,1,2. George Washington Carver: For His Time and Our, Special History Study: *Natural History Related to George Washington Carver National Monument,* Diamond, Missouri.

Carver, George Washington. George Washington Carver Collection, Tuskegee University Archives, Tuskegee, Alabama.

No. 5, 1903, Cow Peas.

No. 21 1911 Experiment Station: White & Color Washing with Native Clays from Macon Co., AL.

No. 22 1912, Experiment Station: Dairying in Connection with Farming.

No. 31, 1925 Experiment Station: How to Grow the Peanut and 101 Ways of Preparing
    it for Human Consumption.

No. 42 1936, Experiment Station: How to Build Up and Maintain the Virgin Fertility
    of Our Soils.

No. 43 1942 Experiment Station: Nature's Garden for Victory & Peace.

Central Avenue Collaborative. "A Brief History of Central Avenue, Historic
    Central Avenue Los Angeles." Last modified July 19, 2015. scalar.usc.edu/works/
    historic-central-avenue-los-angeles/a-brief-history-of-central-avenue.

Cox, Bette Yarbrough. The Negro Directory of Black Los Angeles, CA, 1930–1931. Los
    Angeles: California Eagle Pub. Co., 1930. Retrieved online from calisphere.org/item/
    e8f7d29d3681edbaa8ed1c4ade160fd6/.

Cullen, Countee. My Soul's High Song: The Collected Writings of Countee Cullen. Edited
    by Gerald Early. New York: Anchor Books, 1990.

Dunbar, Paul Laurence. "We Wear the Mask." In The Complete Poems of Paul Laurence
    Dunbar (New York: Dodd, Mead and Company, 1895). Retrieved online www
    .poetryfoundation.org/poems/44203/we-wear-the-mask.

Dunbar-Nelson, Alice. "People of Color in Louisiana: Part II." The Journal of Negro
    History 2, no. 1 (1917): 51–58.

Flamming, Douglas. Bound for Freedom: Black Los Angeles in Jim Crow America. Berkeley:
    University of California Press, 2005.

Fleischman, Lesley, and Marcus Franklin. "Fumes across the Fence-Line: The
    Health Impacts of Air Pollution from Oil & Gas Facilities on African American
    Communities." NCAAP and Clean Air Task Force, November 2017. www.catf.us/
    wpcontent/uploads/2017/11/CATF_Pub_FumesAcrossTheFenceLine.pdf.

Harlan, Louis R., "Desegregation in New Orleans Public Schools During Reconstruction."
    American Historical Review 67, no. 3 (1962): 663–75.

James, David E. The Sons and Daughters of Los: Culture and Community in L.A.
    Philadelphia: Temple University Press, 2003.

Johnson, James Weldon Johnson. The Autobiography of an Ex-Colored Man. New York:
    Dover Publications, 1995.

Kilgallen, Dorothy. "Red Beans and Ricely, Yours," Minneapolis Morning Tribune, March
    7, 1947.

Langlois, Gilles-Antoine. "River of Faith: 300 Years as a New Orleans Catholic
    Community," Clarion Herald, January 8, 2018.

Langlois, Gilles-Antoine. "Tricentennial Thursday: Make That Fleur de Lys, Not the
    Common Fleur de Lis," Clarion Herald, April 30, 2018. clarionherald.org/news/
    tricentennial-thursday-make-that-leur-de-lys-not-the-common-fleur-de-lis.

Lowe, Robert. "The Strange History of School Desegregation," College of Education
    Faculty Research and Publications 88 (2004): n.p.

Menard, John Willis. Lays in Summer Lands. Edited by Larry Eugene Rivers, Richard
    Matthews, and Canter Brown. Tampa: University of Tampa Press, 2002.

McCorkle, James L., Jr. "Los Adaes." In Handbook of Texas Online, Texas State Historical
    Association. Last modified March 1, 1995, www.tshaonline.org/handbook/entries/
    los-adaes.

National Association for the Advancement of Colored People. *Fourth Annual Report, January 1914.* W. E. B. DuBois Papers, MS 312, Special Collections and University Archives, University of Massachusetts Amherst.

National Park Service. "Cultural Landscape Report: Site History, The Oaks, Margaret Murray Washington Period (1915–1925)." *Tuskegee Institute National Historic Site.* Tuskegee, Alabama.

Owens, Maida. "Louisiana's Traditional Cultures: An Overview." In *Swapping Stories: Folktales from Louisiana,* edited by Carl Lindahl, Maida Owens, and C. Renée Harvison, xxix–xlvii. Jackson: University Press of Mississippi, 1997.

Pierce, Jennifer, Mary Mayne, and Barbara Laslett. *Telling Stories: The Use of Personal Narratives in the Social Sciences and History.* New York: Cornell University Press, 2008.

Pollen, Michael. *The Botany of Desire: A Plant's-Eye View of the World.* New York: Random House, 2001.

Sides, Josh. *L.A. City Limits, African American Los Angeles from the Great Depression to the Present.* Berkeley: University of California Press, 2006.

Siler, Charles. "A Commentary: African Cultural Retentions in Louisiana." *Folklife in Louisiana: Louisiana's Living Traditions.* www.louisianafolklife.org/LT/Articles_Essays/afri_cult_retent.html.

"Shreveport Business League Meeting Best of Year," *Shreveport Times,* February 18, 1928, Southern University Library Archive, Shreveport, LA.

Smock, Raymond W., ed. *Booker T. Washington in Perspective: Essays of Louis R. Harlan.* Jackson: University Press of Mississippi, 1988.

Terrell, Mary Church. "The Progress of Colored Women." Address delivered before the National American Women's Suffrage Association, Washington, DC, February 18, 1898, E449 .D16 vol A., no. 13, Daniel Murray Pamphlet Collection and African American Pamphlet Collection, Library of Congress, Washington, DC. www.loc .gov/exhibits/odyssey/educate/terrell.htmlTerrellWritings,1972.

Terrell, Mary Church. "Dr. George Washington Carver of Tuskegee." March 31, 1929, MSS 4249, Box 30 Reel 22, Mary Church Terrell Papers: Speeches and Writings, Library of Congress, Washington, DC. hdl.loc.gov/loc.mss/ms009311.mss42549.0435. Retrieved March 20, 2022.

United States Census Records 1910, Fourth Ward, Shreveport, Caddo Parish, Louisiana, sheet 16. Retrieved from Ancestry.com.

USDA Black Farmers in America, 1865–2000, US Dept of Ag, Rural Business— Cooperative Service, RBS Research Report 194, October 2002.

Williams-Forson, Psyche A. *Building Houses out of Chicken Legs: Black Women, Food, and Power.* Chapel Hill: University of North Carolina Press, 2006.

Y. Yang et al. "Favorite Foods of Older Adults Living in the Black Belt Region of the United States: Influences of Ethnicity, Gender, and Education." *Appetite* 63 (April 2013): 18–23.

ABOUT THE AUTHOR

Photo by Anthony Weaver

Dr. Lizzetta LeFalle-Collins is a distinguished art historian, curator, and writer. She is also a founding staff curator of visual arts at the California African American Museum in Los Angeles, California. Her work has been published in such journals as *Black Renaissance Noire*, *Journal of American Studies*, and *Nka: Journal of Contemporary African Art*. She is also a published storyteller.